Better Learning

Through Structured Teaching

3RD EDITION

DOUGLAS **FISHER**   NANCY **FREY**

Better Learning

Through Structured Teaching

A Framework for the Gradual
Release of Responsibility

3RD EDITION

Alexandria, Virginia USA

1703 N. Beauregard St. • Alexandria, VA 22311-1714 USA
Phone: 800-933-2723 or 703-578-9600 • Fax: 703-575-5400
Website: www.ascd.org • Email: member@ascd.org
Author guidelines: www.ascd.org/write

Ranjit Sidhu, *CEO & Executive Director;* Penny Reinart, *Chief Impact Officer;* Genny Ostertag, *Senior Director, Acquisitions and Editing;* Julie Houtz, *Director, Book Editing;* Katie Martin, *Editor;* Thomas Lytle, *Creative Director;* Donald Ely, *Art Director;* Samantha Wood, *Graphic Designer;* Valerie Younkin, *Senior Production Designer;* Kelly Marshall, *Production Manager;* Christopher Logan, *Senior Production Specialist;* Shajuan Martin, *E-Publishing Specialist*

PAPERBACK ISBN: 978-1-4166-3060-9   ASCD product #121031   n7/21

PDF E-BOOK ISBN: 978-1-4166-3061-6; see Books in Print for other formats.

Quantity discounts are available: email programteam@ascd.org or call 800-933-2723, ext. 5773, or 703-575-5773. For desk copies, go to www.ascd.org/deskcopy.

Library of Congress Cataloging-in-Publication Data
Names: Fisher, Douglas, 1965- author. | Frey, Nancy, 1959- author.
Title: Better learning through structured teaching : a framework for the gradual release of
    responsibility / Douglas Fisher, Nancy Frey.
Description: 3rd edition. | Alexandria, Virginia : ASCD, [2021] | Includes bibliographical references and index.
Identifiers: LCCN 2021015511 (print) | LCCN 2021015512 (ebook) | ISBN 9781416630609
    (paperback) | ISBN 9781416630616 (pdf)
Subjects: LCSH: Active learning. | Teaching. | Constructivism (Education) Classification:
    LCC LB1027.23 .F575 2021 (print) | LCC LB1027.23 (ebook) | DDC 371.3–dc23
LC record available at https://lccn.loc.gov/2021015511
LC ebook record available at https://lccn.loc.gov/2021015512

30 29 28 27 26 25 24 23 22 21   2 3 4 5 6 7 8 9 10 11 12

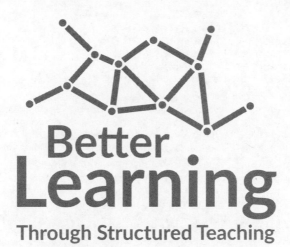

Better Learning
Through Structured Teaching

A Framework for the Gradual
Release of Responsibility

3RD EDITION

Preface to the Third Edition

Who would have thought back in 1999, when we resuscitated and revised the gradual release of responsibility framework, that we would still be adjusting it more than 20 years later? The foundational truths that anchor the two of us, Doug and Nancy, as educators still guide us as much today as they did when we first set out to define effective, intentional instruction. Yet the world continues to change, and we continue to learn, which is why we decided to revise this book for a third edition.

Those who are familiar with past editions may notice some changes. We have updated the chapter on focused instruction based on current thinking about direct instruction and how to ensure that lectures are meaningful. Of course, teacher modeling is still very important, but we know now that there are ways beyond modeling to focus students and ensure that they have strong cognitive apprenticeship experiences. Guided instruction, although far more than simply "telling" or otherwise sharing information, remains an important part of the learning process. You'll find new information about scaffolds that should shape the ways that teachers interact with students to ensure that they are learning during this phase.

Over the past several years, we have also engaged in a great deal of thinking about students' ability to collaborate with their peers, and we drew on work related to professional learning communities to develop the concept of and guidelines for student learning communities. This edition's chapter on collaboration has a great deal of new information on what students gain from working with one another—not just deeper learning and enhanced social-emotional competency but also the awareness that people really do learn more, and learn better, when we learn with others. This chapter also looks at ways that students can collaborate from a distance as they work to negotiate meaning, problem solve, or reach consensus.

In terms of independent learning, we highlight the role of practice much more than we have before. As you will see, practice makes learning permanent, and the evidence on deliberate practice can guide the ways in which students are tasked with completing work. If we can use independent learning for students to preview and review, we might just accelerate their learning and help them reach new levels of success.

New and old readers alike may notice that the examples woven through the chapters include distance and blended learning, informed by lessons learned from teaching during the COVID-19 pandemic. Many of the experiences educators had during this period of mandatory distance learning will serve us well going forward, irrespective of the format of schooling. We have seen the value, for example, in creating interactive videos that provide students information and vocabulary in advance of a lesson.

But the biggest change in this edition is in our approach to assessment—specifically, the point that assessment cannot be "left until the end" of a lesson. Teachers should be adjusting their lessons in real time as they collect and analyze the data that they get from students, whether that be during focused, guided, collaborative, or independent learning. Assessment is the engine that drives instructional decisions; it's what allows teachers to know if we are having an impact. When we are not achieving the desired impact—learning—we have to change course and try something else.

Finally, as we launch into this revised articulation of the gradual release of responsibility framework, we want to remind you just how much teaching matters. The decisions teachers make to structure students' encounters with learning have consequences powerful enough to change lives. Never forget the influence you have on the young people in your classroom. Choose your actions with care. And thank you for all you do, and all you will continue to do, to ensure that learning happens for every student, every day.

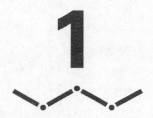

Learning and the Intentional Act of Teaching

As many have noted, teaching is both an art and a science. On the "science" side, there is considerable evidence about the measures proven to support learning that educators can use to inform instructional decisions. We ignore that evidence to our, and our students', peril. Aspects of teaching that fall under the "art" heading include healthy teacher–student relationships, the classroom learning climate, and teachers' passion for the work and their students' learning. This book focuses more on the science of teaching than the art, but you'll read examples that clearly mobilize both art and science.

What's most important is that teaching lead to learning—that it develop in students the knowledge, skill, and confidence they need to learn deeply, think critically and creatively, and be able to apply learning strategies to meet new challenges. If what we are doing is not having that effect, we need to change what we are doing.

The Case for Instructional Frameworks

There is a difference between being prescriptive about instruction and being intentional about it. The purpose of instructional frameworks is not to undercut teacher expertise or professionalism or to tell teachers what to say and how to say it; it's to provide a system of expectations for how students might be taught. Instructional frameworks are a tool that teachers can use to design learning and make informed decisions about the specific strategies that will best support their students' success. In addition, instructional frameworks create a shared vocabulary so that members of teacher teams can communicate more effectively when they interact with one another. Instructional frameworks make it easier to discuss instruction across platforms (face-to-face, distance learning, blended, or hybrid variants). Further, they help teachers identify professional learning opportunities. For example, if one aspect of an instructional framework focuses on student-to-student interaction, teachers might want to learn new ways to enhance this in their classrooms.

Essentially, an instructional framework is a way to organize strategies and deploy them to create cohesive learning experiences for students. It's a defense against the all-too-common and frankly exhausting "buffet model" of professional learning, where teachers are prompted to keep adding to their plates without any idea of where they're going to "put" it all.

A number of instructional frameworks have been developed over the years, but the one we'll be focusing on is called the gradual release of responsibility.

The Gradual Release of Responsibility: A Structure for Supporting Learning

The gradual release of responsibility instructional framework is based on the belief that teachers can intentionally increase students' ownership of learning over time. The framework is informed by several complementary theories, including the following:

- Piaget's (1952) work on cognitive structures and schemata
- Vygotsky's (1962, 1978) work on zones of proximal development
- Bandura's (1965, 2006) work on attention, efficacy, retention, reproduction, and motivation
- Wood, Bruner, and Ross's (1976) work on scaffolded instruction

Taken together, these theories suggest that learning occurs through interactions with others, and being intentional in these interactions allows for specific learning to occur. The mechanism behind the gradual release of responsibility is purposefully shifting the cognitive load from teacher-as-model to joint responsibility of teacher and learner, and then to independent practice and application by the learner (Pearson & Gallagher, 1983). This gradual *decrease* of teacher responsibility and parallel *increase* in student responsibility may occur over a single lesson, a day, a week, a month, or a year.

In the past, interpretations of the gradual release of responsibility limited these interactions to adult and student exchanges: *I do it; We do it together; You do it.* But that three-part model omits a truly vital component of learning: students' collaboration with their peers—the *You do it together* phase. Thus, our interpretation of the gradual release of responsibility framework includes four major phases. In Figure 1.1, we map out these phases of learning, indicating the share of responsibility that students and teachers have in each.

We are not suggesting that every lesson must always start with focused instruction (goal setting and modeling) before progressing to guided instruction, then to collaborative learning, and finally to independent tasks. Teachers can and often do reorder the phases—for example, beginning a lesson with an independent task, such as bell work or a quick-write, or engaging students in collaborative peer inquiry prior to providing teacher modeling. As we stress throughout this book, what is important and necessary for deep learning is that students experience all four phases of learning when encountering new content. We will explore the four phases in greater detail in subsequent chapters, but let's proceed now with an overview of each.

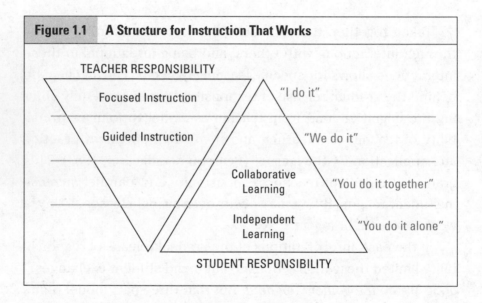

Figure 1.1   A Structure for Instruction That Works

Focused Instruction

This phase includes two components: establishing the purpose for learning—that is, setting learning intentions and success criteria—and providing cognitive apprenticeship opportunities through modeling and demonstration. In focused instruction (which, as noted, does not have to come at the beginning of a lesson), students get to know what they are learning and see examples of the type of thinking that they are expected to do. Here are some examples of what teachers and learners might be doing during the focused instruction phase:

Teacher Actions	Student Actions
• Describing the learning intentions and success criteria • Noting the relevance of the lesson • Thinking aloud, demonstrating, or providing direct instruction	• Listening and making connections • Taking notes or talking with a partner about what the class is learning • Developing a mental model of expertise

Focused instruction is typically done with the whole class and usually lasts 15 minutes or less—long enough to clearly establish purpose and ensure that students have a model from which to work. Bear in mind, too, that there is no reason to limit focused instruction to once per lesson. The gradual release of responsibility instructional framework is recursive, and a teacher might reassume responsibility several times during a lesson to reestablish the lesson purpose and provide additional examples of expert thinking.

Guided Instruction

The guided instruction phase is an opportunity to scaffold students' understanding. Through the use of questions, prompts, and cues, teachers can support student learning without telling them answers or simply providing them with information. Guided instruction can be done with a whole class, but many teachers are more effective when they guide small, purposeful groups that have been composed based on assessment data. Here are some examples of what teachers and learners might be doing during the guided instruction phase:

Teacher Actions	Student Actions
• Asking questions • Scaffolding with prompts, cues, and direct explanations • Meeting with intentionally selected groups of students • Monitoring progress and documenting learning	• Responding to the teacher's questions • Thinking and noticing, based on the scaffolds • Experiencing productive success with the support of the teacher

Guided instruction is an ideal time to differentiate learning experiences by varying the instructional materials used, the level of prompting or questioning employed, and the products expected. A single guided instructional event won't translate into all students developing the content knowledge or skills they are lacking, but a series of guided instructional events can. Over time and with cues, prompts, and questions, teachers can guide students to increasingly complex thinking. Guided instruction is, in part, about establishing high expectations and providing students with the support they need to reach those expectations.

Collaborative Learning

The collaborative learning phase of instruction is too often neglected. If used at all, it tends to be a "special event" rather than an established instructional routine. When done right, collaborative learning is a way for students to consolidate their thinking and expand their understanding. Negotiating with peers, discussing ideas and information, problem solving, and engaging in inquiry with others give students the opportunity to use what they have learned during focused and guided instruction. Here are some examples of what teachers and learners might be doing during the collaborative learning phase:

Teacher Actions	Student Actions
• Developing complex tasks • Forming groups purposefully • Assigning roles • Monitoring progress	• Using academic language in interactions with peers • Sharing opinions, ideas, and thoughts • Problem solving and using argumentation • Working to achieve consensus

Because collaborative learning situations help students think through key ideas, they are a natural opportunity for inquiry and a way to promote engagement with the content. As such, they are critical to the successful implementation of the gradual release of responsibility instructional framework. Note, though, that collaborative learning is not the time to introduce new information to students. This phase of instruction is a time for students to apply what they already know in novel situations or engage in a spiral review of previous knowledge.

Independent Learning

The ultimate goal of instruction is that students be able to independently apply information, ideas, content, skills, and strategies in unique situations. We want to create learners who are not reliant on others for information and ideas. As such, students need practice completing independent tasks and learning from those tasks. Overall and across time, the school and instructional events must be "organized to encourage and support a continued, increasingly mature and comprehensive acceptance of responsibilities for one's own learning" (Kesten, 1987, p. 15). The effectiveness of independent learning, however, depends on students' readiness to engage in it; too many students are asked to complete independent tasks without having received the focused or guided instruction they need to do so successfully. Here are some examples of what teachers and learners might be doing during the independent learning phase:

Teacher Actions	Student Actions
• Developing practice and application tasks • Monitoring student progress	• Completing assignments • Planning and monitoring their own efforts • Reflecting on their own successes

When students are ready to apply skills and knowledge, there is a range of independent tasks that might be used. Our experience suggests that the more authentic a task is, the more likely the student is to complete it. For example, a kindergarten teacher might ask a student to read a familiar book to three adults, a 6th grade science teacher might ask a student to predict the outcome of a lab based on the previous three experiments, and a high school art teacher might ask a student to incorporate light and perspective into a new painting. What's essential for an independent learning task is that it clearly relate to the instruction each student has received yet also provide the student an opportunity to apply the resulting knowledge in a new way.

Structures That Don't Support Learning

With this effective approach to instruction fresh in mind, let's look at some structures that don't support learning nearly as well. Unfortunately, there are still plenty of classrooms in which responsibility for learning is *not* being transferred from knowledgeable others (teachers, peers, parents) to students. Although they may feature some of the phases of instruction we have described, the omission of other phases derails learning in significant ways.

For example, in some classrooms, teachers provide explanations and then skip straight to asking students to complete independent tasks—an approach graphically represented in Figure 1.2. This situation is very familiar. A teacher demonstrates how to approach a particular kind of algebra problem and then asks students to solve the odd-numbered problems in the back of the book. A teacher reads a text aloud and then asks students to complete a comprehension worksheet based on the reading. In both cases, the teacher fails to develop students' understanding of the content through the purposeful interaction of guided instruction. This is a sudden release of responsibility, not a gradual one. It's a structure that favors students who arrive already knowing the content. Students who are not yet proficient with the content suffer in this environment, because they lack sufficient scaffolding to learn.

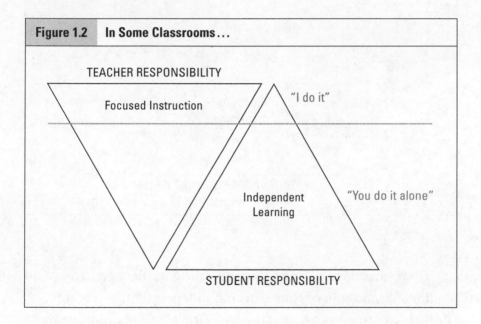

Figure 1.2   In Some Classrooms...

TEACHER RESPONSIBILITY

Focused Instruction

"I do it"

Independent Learning

"You do it alone"

STUDENT RESPONSIBILITY

Sadly, there is a classroom model even worse than this, at least in terms of instructional development. It's the one in which students are asked to learn everything on their own, depicted in Figure 1.3. The structure of these classes is depressingly uniform. Students complete the prepared study packet of photocopied worksheets or online tasks, or they read the assigned pages and then answer the questions at the back of the textbook. Then they follow this pattern over and over again, day after day. There really isn't much teaching going on in these classrooms; it's mostly assigning or *causing* work. This is do-it-yourself school, and frankly, we'd be embarrassed to accept our paychecks if we "taught" like this.

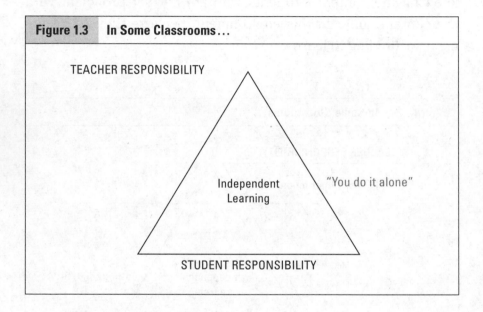

Figure 1.3   In Some Classrooms...

TEACHER RESPONSIBILITY

Independent Learning

"You do it alone"

STUDENT RESPONSIBILITY

There are days at school when students do need to spend significant amounts of time working independently—completing projects, writing essays, and the like. However, this should not be happening every day, and on the days it does happen, students need to be reminded of the purpose of the lesson, experience a brief episode of expert thinking, and interact with their peers.

Even in classrooms that most people would consider "good" or "good enough," the gradual release of responsibility instructional framework is seldom fully operationalized. As noted, the most frequent omission is the collaborative learning phase, leading to the instructional approach represented in Figure 1.4.

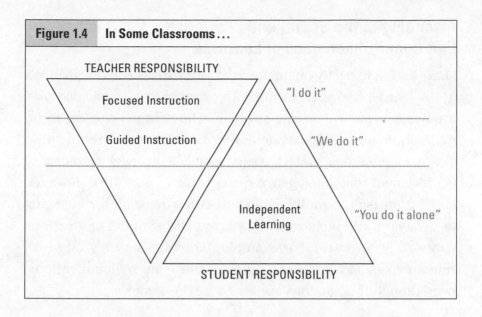

Figure 1.4   In Some Classrooms...

TEACHER RESPONSIBILITY

Focused Instruction   "I do it"

Guided Instruction   "We do it"

Independent   "You do it alone"
Learning

STUDENT RESPONSIBILITY

In these classrooms, the teacher provides modeling and then meets with small groups of students. But students don't have the opportunity to collaborate, as they are all required to complete independent tasks while waiting their turn to meet with the teacher. For example, the teacher might model comprehension strategies useful in understanding scientific texts (*I do it*) and then meet with two or three small groups of students to guide their understanding (*We do it together*). As this is going on, the rest of the students are more likely to be assigned independent reading from a textbook (*You do it alone*) than they are to work in collaborative learning groups (*You do it together*).

We believe that all four phases of the gradual release of responsibility framework—focused instruction, guided instruction, collaborative learning, and independent learning—are necessary if we want students to learn deeply, think critically and creatively, and be able to mobilize learning strategies.

Attending to the Social and Emotional Dimensions of Learning

Learning isn't strictly an intellectual enterprise. The dispositions of the learner and that learner's investment in learning also play a powerful role in learning success. The extensive research on motivation in learning has demonstrated that self-determination matters a great deal. In fact, motivation is a stronger predictor of achievement than intelligence (Kriegbaum et al., 2018). However, motivation isn't monolithic, and people's reasons for engaging in behaviors can include both internal and external motivations (Howard et al., 2017). For example, individuals on a group bike ride are likely to represent a range of these internal motivations, even though their actions appear to be the same:

- "I have to do this." (I exercise because my doctor says I must.)
- "I can do this." (I am capable of riding a bike for 40 miles.)
- "I want to do this." (I like the way bike riding makes me feel physically and mentally.)

Our classrooms are likewise filled with students possessing a range of motivations. Because of motivation's complexity, we've found it helpful to think of a learner's motivation as being informed by three factors: *identity, agency,* and *self-regulation.*

Identity as a learner. Identity is an understanding of who we are. Our attributes, which is to say our *characteristics,* are informed by the way the world reacts to us. Young children learn about themselves relative to their interactions with others and align their responses to be consistent with those of their caregivers. A young child encounters a strange dog and looks to the adult holding his hand to see whether he should be afraid or not. This experience becomes a story he can tell about himself: "I saw a big dog, but Mama said I was brave because I didn't act scared."

A person's identity is further informed by fixed and fluid structures such as gender, race, sexual orientation, culture, and socioeconomic status. Societal messages can both enhance and inhibit a child's learning. Consider that the phenomenon of stereotype threat has a documented negative influence, with a measured effect equivalent to a year's loss of learning. A learning environment in which students perceive that a negative performance on their part will reinforce a negative stereotype about an affiliated group puts these students at risk. Their anxiousness about doing well actually reduces their performance. Stereotype threat has been documented in children as young as 1st grade (Désert et al., 2009). However, classroom instruction that incorporates exposure to positive messages about affiliated groups can help to create "stereotype boost" in these same children, enhancing their performance (Shih et al., 2012). We would be remiss if this book about instruction overlooked the importance of culturally relevant and culturally sustaining pedagogies in the learning lives of students.

Agency in learning. A person's sense of agency is closely linked to personal identity. *Agency* is one's perceived capacity to take action in the world. It is socially constructed and influenced by the network of relationships a child has at home and at school.

It's fair to say that agency is at the heart of the gradual release of responsibility instructional framework; after all, the framework is constructed to ensure that students have frequent opportunities to take calculated learning risks as they continually try on new knowledge and skills. Students with a higher degree of agency have the confidence necessary to step beyond reception and toward action, working through problems alone and with others, testing solutions, and reflecting on their results in order to innovate and improve on their attempts. At the same time, it is by successfully assuming responsibility, within the guardrails of the framework, that students build greater agency.

Of course, successful assumption of responsibility depends on the teacher's successful release of it. A teacher who overestimates the value of telling and fails to provide chances for students to try on new thinking thwarts their ability to develop agency in their learning. That teacher breeds a dependency and signals to children that learning is a one-way proposition: *I tell, and you listen.* This sets up learning as a passive experience rather than one that requires action and effort. Under these circumstances, is it any wonder that many students fail to recognize their own motivation as a critical part of the learning equation?

Self-regulation in learning. *Self-regulation* is a collective term that describes the habits, dispositions, and skills students need to "learn how to learn." Individuals who can self-regulate are able to direct their attention, organize their thinking, and make decisions about what they need to do next.

One important dimension of self-regulation is *metacognition,* which is thinking about one's thinking. It was once assumed that only older children could engage in metacognitive thinking. We know now that children as young as age 3 can reflect on a task and tell you what steps they must take to complete it. Further, they can describe, after the task is over, what actions would have made it easier (Marulis et al., 2016). Metacognitive abilities are accelerated when students have opportunities to reflect on their learning, which is required in all phases of the gradual release of responsibility instructional framework.

Persistence in tasks is another disposition important in the development of self-regulation. The ability to stick with a task even when it is difficult has a developmental component to it, but like metacognition, we see evidence of this at a surprisingly early age. Students who have strong persistence can direct, and redirect, their attention. They decide to continue working and thinking, in part because they have experienced success doing so in the past, and in part because others have recognized their efforts to stay focused on the learning. They also grasp the restorative value of taking a little break before returning to a vexing task.

The X Factor in Instructional Success: Teacher Credibility

There is plenty of evidence about what works best to ensure academic learning and social-emotional development. But the same strategies can get different outcomes, based on the *credibility* the teacher has established with students.

The research points to four components of teacher credibility that play a significant role in students' growth: *trust, competence, dynamism,* and *immediacy.* Thankfully, there are specific actions teachers can take to increase personal credibility in each of these areas.

Trust

Students want to know that their teachers really care about them as individuals and have their best academic and social interests at heart. Students also want to know that their teachers are reliable and true to their word. First, a few general points about trust:

- If you make a promise, work to keep it, or explain why you could not.
- Tell students the truth about their performance; they know when their work is below standard and wonder why you are telling them otherwise.
- Don't spend all your time trying to catch students in "bad behavior," yet be honest about the impact that their behavior has on you as an individual.
- Examine any negative feelings you have about specific students; they sense it, and it compromises the trust within the classroom.

Competence

This aspect of teacher credibility is the main focus of this book. Students expect an appropriate level of expertise from their teachers in terms of delivery and accuracy of information. In other words, they want teachers to know their stuff and know how to teach that stuff. Students expect lessons to be well paced and effective, and they expect the information you provide to be accurate. To build recognizable competence...

- Make sure you know the content well; this kind of preparation requires advance planning. Be honest when a question arises that you are not sure how to answer.
- Organize lesson delivery in a cohesive and coherent way.
- Consider how your nonverbal behaviors communicate competence, such as the position of your hands when you talk with students or your facial expressions. Students notice defensive positions and indications that you are dismissing or don't value their comments or contributions.

Dynamism

This aspect of teacher credibility focuses on the passion teachers bring to the classroom and the content they teach. Dynamism is really about the ability to communicate enthusiasm—for subject matter and for students' learning. It's also about developing lessons capable of capturing students' interest. To increase dynamism...

- Remind yourself why you wanted to be a teacher and what aspects of the content you love. Students notice when their teachers are bored by what they're teaching. (We think "Make content interesting!" is a motto all teachers should adopt.)
- Consider the relevance of your lessons. Does the content lend itself to application outside the classroom? Do

students have opportunities to learn about themselves and their problem-solving abilities? Does the content link in some way to civic engagement or provide opportunities for tangible community action? When students don't see the relevance of their assignments, they check out; you may get compliance, but you will not get committed learning.

- Seek feedback from trusted colleagues about your lesson delivery. Ask those colleagues to focus more on the passion you bring to lesson content than on the individual strategies you use. Students respond to passion and energy in a lesson, even when they didn't think they would be interested.

Immediacy

This final construct of teacher credibility focuses on how accessible students perceive the teacher to be—the immediacy of the teacher's attention and responses. Teachers who make themselves accessible, who move around the room and work to be easy to connect with and relate to, signal to students that their learning is a priority. To improve your immediacy...

- Get to know your students as people. Students easily detect when you're indifferent to their interests and passions; it communicates to them that you're not invested in them or their overall success.
- Attend extracurricular events so that students see you outside the familiar classroom setting. Even the most skeptical students will notice you're there and think about your presence.
- Teach with urgency, but not to the point that the classroom climate becomes stressful. Students want to know that their learning matters and that you are not wasting

their time, but they also want to be pulled into the feeling that the work is important and worth their investment rather than something imposed on them.

- Start the class on time and use every minute wisely. This means preparing tasks that students can complete while you engage in routine work like taking attendance. It means having a series of "sponge activities" ready when lessons run short. Students notice when time is wasted. Lots of "free time" communicates to them that neither the content nor their learning is a high priority.

Take a moment to think about how these aspects of teacher credibility encompass both art and science. As noted previously, this book focuses mainly on the intentional use of instructional strategies that deepen student learning and develop students' learning capacity. Over several decades' worth of experience and research, we have come to believe that planning and delivering lessons with the gradual release of responsibility instructional framework enhances teacher competency and, thus, teacher credibility.

Conclusion

The gradual release of responsibility framework is a structure that requires teachers to commit to the following:

- Knowing their students and content well
- Regularly assessing students' understanding of the content
- Purposefully planning lessons that transfer responsibility from the teacher to the student in order to build student identity and agency by equipping them with the self-regulation skills they need to fuel their own learning

In the remainder of this book, we examine each aspect of this instructional framework and note how intentionally structuring learning experiences helps teachers meet students' needs and develop both students' confidence and competence and their own.

2

Focused Instruction: Purpose and Cognitive Apprenticeship

Learning through apprenticeship has occurred throughout human history. Young people learned a trade at the side of an expert adult and engaged in years of experiences that included observation, practice and feedback, and reflection. Expert adults framed these experiences by sharing their thinking about the process, demonstrating techniques, and debriefing the results. Purpose was at the center of apprenticeship: learners could see the reasons for what they were being asked to learn and how the pieces fit together.

Of course, most of us are not teaching students how to make horseshoes, weave a tapestry, or repair air conditioning systems (to use a modern example). What's more, the concepts and skills we teach are largely abstract. Teachers today are less "dispensers of knowledge" than facilitators of inquiry, reasoning, and argumentation. We know that if we want our students to engage in critical thinking, we must be critical thinkers ourselves. The gradual release of responsibility is, as a whole, an expression of the cognitive apprenticeship model, and cognitive apprenticeship is an explicit feature of the focused instruction phase.

As described by Collins and colleagues (1989), the purpose of cognitive apprenticeship in schooling is to make implicit processes—like critical thinking and reasoning—visible to learners. This can be achieved via modeling and demonstration that is accompanied by coaching and scaffolding. Collins and colleagues also note the importance of articulation—that is, of separating complex skills into more digestible parts before reconsolidating them as the whole. In cognitive apprenticeship, a teacher prompts students to compare their thinking to the thinking of others; this is another step on the path to developing internalized expertise. Note that the thinking of others includes the teacher's thinking (accessed via modeling/thinking aloud) *and* the thinking of "experts" (accessed, say, via textbooks or original sources).

A learner who sees a new skill executed, a new strategy deployed, or a new concept applied has a better sense of its value and more impetus to master it. In this chapter, we examine the instructional moves that focus students on the learning at hand. These instructional moves—*establishing purpose* and *cognitive apprenticeships*—are vital in preparing students for successful learning.

Although the focused instruction phase is often brief in nature, it is powerful—the time when the teacher uses the students' attention to introduce the concept, skill, or strategy they are to learn and executes key instructional steps necessary to make what is being taught transparent to the learner. This notion of transparency is critical in focused instruction. As noted, in order for students to acquire new knowledge, they need to understand its purpose and the learning target. They need to witness a more knowledgeable other (typically, the teacher) direct his or her own thinking, and they need to be invited into the mind of that more knowledgeable other. Teachers issue this invitation by clarifying for students not only the overall task process but also how to tackle the decisions they must make to complete the task successfully. Finally, students need a knowledgeable teacher who will closely observe their early attempts and continue to support their learning success.

The Value of Focused Instruction

Focused instruction is not the time when a teacher simply *tells* students things—in fact, there's no time in teaching when "just telling" is enough. The key to quality teaching is *explaining*. Students need an explanation of their teachers' cognitive processes and metacognitive thinking. Focused instruction is a way for learners to encounter both the content and the internal thinking and decision making that occur as experts share their cognitive processes.

Because this phase is relatively short, it can be tempting to hurry through it, dispensing some facts and doling out some directions. As one teacher asked, "Do we always need to give students a reason for everything? Shouldn't they just have to read because we told them to?" Although the "just because" reason can be enough if the desired outcome is compliance, the goal of school should always be learning. Telling students *what* they will be doing but not *why, how, when,* and *when not* presumes a tremendous amount of motivation, self-regulation, and skill. Some students may learn well enough without *whys, hows, whens,* and *when nots,* but many more will not.

Establishing Purpose

One of the major roles of focused instruction is to establish a purpose for learning. In the absence of explicit attention to the lesson's purpose, students will not see the connection between the activities they are completing (the tasks listed on the agenda) and the reasons why they are learning it (how, when, and where to apply it). Short and colleagues (2012) note that establishing purpose is especially critical to the success of English language learners. When students are just learning the language their teacher is speaking, they don't always know what to pay attention to in class and which points really matter.

Unfortunately, in many districts, the good idea of establishing purpose has been misapplied and reduced to the requirement that teachers post the learning targets (or worse, the standards) associated with the lesson on the board or learning management system. Simply posting these will not make the purpose clear to students. Students need to be involved in the process of establishing purpose, they need to talk about the purpose, and they need to understand the goals of the instruction.

Teachers can establish purpose in three domains: content, language, and social. Consider the following example. A 4th grade teacher established purpose right after her students had responded to a writing prompt posted as their bell work. The prompt read, "When a little kid asks me about a food chain, here's how I will explain it...." Then the teacher said this:

As you know or could predict from our writing prompt, we're still studying the food chain. Today, we're going to look at the primary source of matter and energy in the food chain—plants. We need to learn more about plants as a source of matter and energy so that we can understand the food chain better. In doing so, I want to be sure that we're paying attention to our key terms: *producers* and *consumers* such as *herbivores, carnivores, omnivores,* and *decomposers*. I also want to make sure that we remember to write in complete sentences, not fragments. And finally, our social goal for the week is to actively listen while others are speaking. To accomplish these things, I'll be reading and talking about plants with you, and then you'll be reading, talking, and writing about them as well. Some of you will be doing research; others will be reading more about decomposers such as fungi, insects, and microorganisms that recycle matter from dead plants and animals; and still others will be watching a short film about this topic.

Notice where establishing purpose occurred in the lesson: *after* students had engaged in some independent learning. Keep in mind that the instructional moves we make in a gradual release of responsibility instructional framework are not strictly linear. An established purpose makes checking for understanding clearer, as both the students and the teacher know what will be accepted as evidence of learning for that lesson. It also serves as a means for reminding students what the learning targets are as they transition to another phase of the lesson, reducing the chances that they lose the reason for learning because they're attending to the activity directions. Finally, a return to the established purpose is a way of closing the lesson. It underscores all that's gone before.

Providing Apprenticeship Experiences

Once students understand what they are learning and what successful learning looks like, they are ready for *apprenticeship experiences*, which can include modeling and demonstrating, direct instruction, or even lectures. A teacher's intentional approach to these instructional staples makes all the difference in effectiveness.

Modeling and Demonstrating with Think-Alouds

We think of *modeling* as an instructional move to use when the lesson addresses using a cognitive process, such as reading, writing, or mathematics. *Demonstrating* is a good choice when focusing on physical tasks, such as the proper stance for swinging a baseball bat or the procedure for turning on a Bunsen burner.

Think of the times you have viewed an online video demonstration of a complicated process you were interested in learning. Whether it was a video on how to make a soufflé or the basic casts in fly fishing, it was most likely accompanied by the narration of an expert who explained what he or she was doing. The combination of verbal and visual elements reinforces the important aspects of the task. The features of modeling and demonstrating are similar. Here they are, accompanied by an example of how a language arts teacher might model and think aloud about the process of sentence combining:

1. *Name the strategy, skill, or task.* ("Today I am going to show you how to combine sentences to make more interesting and complex statements.")

2. *State the purpose of the strategy, skill, or task.* ("It's important for a writer to be able to construct sentences that aren't repetitive or choppy. Sentence combining is one way to make sure your sentences read more smoothly.")

3. *Explain when the strategy or skill is used.* ("After I have written a passage, I reread it to see if I have choppy sentences or if I am repeating information unnecessarily. When I notice that's occurred, I look for ways to combine sentences.")

4. *Use analogies to link prior knowledge to new learning.* ("I like to think of this as making sure I make a straight path for my readers to follow. When I eliminate choppy or redundant sentences, it's like making a straight path of ideas for them to follow.")

5. *Demonstrate how the skill, strategy, or task is completed.* ("I'm going to show you three short, choppy sentences. I'll look first for information I can cross out because it is repetitive. Then I'm going to combine those three sentences into one longer and more interesting sentence.")

6. *Alert learners about errors to avoid.* ("I have to be careful not to cut out so much information that I lose the meaning. I also need to watch out for sentences that become too long. A reader can lose the meaning of a sentence that's too long.")
7. *Assess the use of the skill.* ("Now I'm going to reread my new sentence to see if it makes sense.")

Done right, modeling or demonstrating is more than simply "showing," because there is an accompanying spoken narrative for the learner to follow. When learners have a concept, skill, or strategy modeled and explained, they gain a deeper understanding for when to apply it, what to watch out for, and how to analyze their success. This is consistent with four dimensions of learning: declarative (*What is it?*), procedural (*How do I use it?*), conditional (*When and where do I use it?*), and reflective (*How do I know I used it correctly?*) (Atkinson & Shiffrin, 1968). You can also see elements of metacognition emerging in the modeling example. Students are not just being taught how to do something; they are being primed to analyze the success of their use of what they are learning. Consider recording some of the modeling you do and posting these video files on your learning management system for students to return to if they need a skill refresher.

Demonstrations are similarly appropriate for tasks that involve movement, coordination, or any complex physical component. As an example, consider the approach Brenda Lattner* uses to begin a watercolor painting unit with her middle school art class. She knows her students need to learn how to stretch their watercolor paper correctly in order to have a satisfactory result with their final product. She starts by naming all the

---

*All the teachers and students we discuss in this book are real people, with names changed to protect their privacy.

materials she will need for the task, including the paper, art tape, clean water, two sponges, and a board for mounting the paper. Next, she talks through the process:

> The first thing I need to do is check to make sure I have the side of the paper I want to use facing up. I can paint on either side, but I like to use the rougher side of the paper because it seems to hold my paint better. I can run my hand over both sides of the paper to figure out which side is rougher. The paper needs to soak in the water for a few minutes, so I am going to place it in the pan and set the timer for three minutes. That way I won't forget. In the pan, I put *tepid* water, which means water that is around room temperature. Hot water can ruin the paper. While it is soaking, I'll cut the strips of tape I'll need to mount the paper on the board. I have to make sure that the tape isn't shorter than the length of each side. If it is, the paper will dry funny, and I'll have a big bubble in it.

After the timer rings, Ms. Lattner continues:

> I'm going to be careful as I lift the paper, because I want as much water as possible to drain off of it. I can't put a sopping wet paper on the board because it will take forever to dry.

She holds the paper above the pan to allow the excess water to drain, explaining what she is thinking and doing:

> OK, I think that's as much water as I'm going to get off of the paper this way. I've been watching the amount of water dripping in the pan, and it has slowed down to almost nothing. I know I can get water off another way: I'm going to lay the paper down on the board and use this sponge to smooth it. I've checked the sponge to make sure it's clean, and now I'm going to run it across the paper, using long strokes. The sponge absorbs water as it smooths the paper. Now that the paper is smooth, I need to tape it down. This tape gets sticky on one side, but you need

water to make it sticky. I use a brown sponge for wetting the tape, so that I never mix up my smoothing sponges with my taping ones. You know why? Because that sticky stuff from the tape gets on the sponge. If I accidentally use that sponge later for smoothing, I'll get it all over the paper, and the paper will be ruined.

Ms. Lattner places the tape on all four edges of the paper, affixes it to the wooden board, and continues:

Now it's done! It needs to dry overnight, and when I check it tomorrow, it will be very tight and smooth. As the paper dries, it contracts, which means it gets a bit smaller. The tape holds it in place, so the contraction of the paper stretches it tight. When I paint on it, the surface will be smooth, and it won't crinkle up as I apply the watercolors to it.

This demonstration includes not only the sequence of steps but also insight into how to decide when it's time to go on to the next step. You may have noticed Ms. Lattner carefully noting the errors to avoid when completing this task. These verbal protocols, more commonly called *think-alouds,* are a common feature of focused instruction. They are not stream-of-consciousness monologues but intentional narration of the decision-making processes used in the moment, designed to bring your modeling alive by drawing learners into your thinking.

Duffy (2009) refers to think-alouds as "letting [students] in on the secret" to successfully completing a task (p. 50). They give students the opportunity to witness how an expert merges declarative, procedural, conditional, and reflective knowledge in a fluent fashion.

There are five important considerations in crafting an effective think-aloud: brevity, metacognition, authenticity, expertise, and specificity. Here are some guidelines we recommend (Fisher & Frey, 2019):

Keep the think-aloud brief. It is easy to get carried away with a think-aloud and turn it into a rambling monologue of every thought that wanders through your head. Choose a short piece of written text, a single math word problem, or one example of a procedure. It is better to deliver a short but effective think-aloud than one that serves only to confuse the learner with too many details.

Pay attention to your own thinking processes as you design your think-aloud. This is really very difficult when you are an expert at something. Nathan and Petrosino (2003) state that "well-developed subject matter knowledge can lead people to assume that learning should follow the structure of the subject-matter domain rather than the learning needs and developmental profiles of novices"—a phenomenon they call the "expert blind spot" (p. 909). In other words, when you've been very adept at something for a long time, it can be difficult to retrace your own learning footsteps to recall a time when this information was new to you. A successful think-aloud requires you to engage in advance metacognition: unpack your own thinking processes to understand how you arrive at understanding. What skills are you using? What habits of mind?

Find your authentic voice. Think-alouds require lots of "I" statements, which can feel contrived when you first begin. As teachers, it seems more comfortable to tell students information, using lots of "you" statements. The problem with "you" state-ments is that they shift instruction to direct explanation rather than making expert thinking transparent. Another caution is to resist adopting an overly authoritative tone. Use academic vocab-ulary, but talk like yourself. Your students will find it more help-ful to hear you say, "Wow—when I first looked at this diagram of the solar system, I thought right away about what it didn't have in the illustration, like the asteroid belt and the dwarf planets," rather than "I analyzed the diagram for the visual information it contained and immediately noted the small solar system bodies it did not contain."

Think like the expert you are. Keeping a think-aloud authentic doesn't mean you have to check your expertise at the door. As a content-area expert, you have the ability to share unique insights with your students. Effective think-alouds give you the opportunity to think like the mathematician, scientist, artist, historian, athlete, or literary critic you are, in front of your students.

Name your cognitive and metacognitive processes. Labeling is essential if students are to build their own metacognitive awareness. Tell students when you are using the associative property of multiplication or sourcing a primary source document in a history class; these are cognitive approaches you are teaching them to use. In addition, signal your own metacognition as you solve problems ("OK, that didn't work, so I have to try a different formula"), acquire new knowledge ("Wow, that's something I didn't know until just now, reading this article"), and regulate your learning ("I know that I usually understand an editorial better when I know who's written it, so I always look at the writer's affiliation first").

Modeling with a think-aloud is often done in conjunction with the kind of text analysis associated with close reading. Many teachers project the reading so that students can follow along as the text is read. Others provide students with their own digital or paper copy of the reading. Regardless of the way in which students access the text, it is the teacher who is doing the reading while students follow along silently. The teacher pauses throughout the reading to think aloud about the information and to explain their own mental processes in understanding the text.

Now, an example. Craig Brownlee, a 10th grade biology teacher, has been teaching a unit about the human immune response, and his students have been struggling with understanding the role of phagocytes in fighting disease. He reads a passage aloud: "Phagocytes destroy any foreign body, including the debris and dead cells produced by injury. They overwhelm the injured areas and engulf the foreign bodies through a process called phagocytosis." Mr. Brownlee knows this statement contains a number of concepts that are easily misunderstood, so he pauses to think aloud:

> When I first learned about phagocytes, I couldn't really get my head around what they did. Then my biology professor told me that *phagocyte* means "a cell that eats." That helped me understand a bit more. A phagocyte doesn't eat like we do, but it swallows up the garbage that shouldn't be there. There's a word in that sentence that confirms my recollection of that idea. The word *engulf* means "to swallow something up," "to surround it." Now I can connect that to one more idea in that sentence— phagocytosis. Anytime I see a word that ends in *-osis,* it's a signal to me that it is a process. So phagocytosis is the process used by a phagocyte, a cell that eats, to swallow up anything it thinks shouldn't belong there. I had to take that sentence apart to understand it, and I did it by analyzing the derivations of a science term, then confirming my understanding using other terms in the sentence.

Here, Mr. Brownlee is modeling how he understands this informational text as a biologist. He also is explicit in naming the strategies he activated, so as not to leave it to chance whether his students would notice (or not). Keep in mind that one goal of the think-aloud is to let novices in on how an expert synthesizes skills and habits of mind. Another is to prime students to become more aware of their own thinking processes. This metacognitive awareness is essential in order for students to gain insight into their own learning, and it is invaluable during guided instruction and collaborative learning, when students are required to express their thinking in words.

It's important to keep in mind that modeling or demonstrating with think-alouds is not meant to be an extended monologue; in practice, take care to regularly punctuate your demonstrations with student interaction. Invite students to ask questions, to speculate, and to make connections. Their contributions provide a window on their understanding, including any misconceptions you'll need to address. This formative function of modeling is one reason why we encourage teachers to use it throughout a lesson and not restrict it to the introduction of new information.

Direct Instruction

Direct instruction is a useful instructional tool for introducing new information to learners. It relies on a teacher's explanation of the skill or strategy to be used, followed by first breaking it down into smaller steps and then linking the elements together into a larger whole.

A common misconception about direct instruction is that it's didactic and focuses solely on the teacher, with little participation by students. But direct instruction, done well, includes periodic checking for understanding, practice in the company of the teacher, and scaffolding. As summarized in Rosenshine's (2008) review of the research, teachers can boost the effectiveness of direct instruction by doing the following:

- Reducing the difficulty of the task during initial practice by stating lesson goals and dividing the task into smaller components.
- Using scaffolds and guidance to support students during initial practice. The teacher models, thinks aloud as strategies are selected and choices are made, anticipates errors, checks for understanding, obtains responses from all students, and gradually combines the components into a whole.

- Providing supportive feedback, including systematic corrections, checklists, models of the completed task, and fix-up strategies.

Direct instruction is widely used in every subject and for learners of all ages, and for good reason: it has real potential to accelerate learning. As reported by the Visible Learning database (www.visiblelearningmetax.com), the effect size of direct instruction is 0.59, well above the 0.40 effect size average for the 250 documented influences on student learning. Direct instruction follows a pattern familiar to effective educators: introduce new learning, link it to what students already know, and provide opportunities for practice.

Consider this example. Sixth grade English teacher Robin Miller is introducing a unit on argumentative writing to her students. They haven't had prior experience with this form of writing, and her goal is to build a bridge between a more familiar writing technique—writing to express opinion—and this new one. Ms. Miller begins by establishing the purpose of the lesson: *to learn about the characteristics of argumentation*. She introduces the term and discusses the root word *argument* as a starting point. "When someone has a good argument, they make points that their opponent can understand. The goal is to get someone to agree with you," she says. "You want them to change their mind." Ms. Miller asks her students what kinds of things they argue for or against in their families. The students immediately brighten up, and their ideas come quickly: getting a pet, doing chores, screen time, having the remote control. Ms. Miller records all these contributions and says, "I like these ideas. Now let's consider what makes a winning argument."

The teacher introduces characteristics of argumentative writing. "A good argument is based on facts," she says. "We call those facts *evidence*. The evidence has to be truthful and accurate.

If you were arguing to get a pet, for example, you couldn't just make up evidence."

Ms. Miller tells the class she has an argument for getting a pet that she'd like them to review. She distributes a short piece of text, then asks them to read it and underline the facts the writer used. Her students find facts about the overpopulation of strays and the number of pet adoptions in the community. "These facts are evidence," she stresses. "Go ahead and label those statements as evidence in the margin."

Ms. Miller continues, "A good argument gets right to the point. We call that a *claim*." She continues with further explanation about what makes for a good claim, then redirects her students back to the short passage. "Can you find the claim in here?" she prompts. "What does this writer want? When you find that statement, underline it and label it as the claim."

Her final teaching point in this direct instruction lesson on argumentative writing focuses on the counterclaim. "A good argument anticipates what the other person might say to challenge your claim," Ms. Miller says. "Have you heard the expression that 'the best defense is a good offense'?" Several students begin offering their experiences playing organized sports. "Yes, exactly!" says the teacher. "In a written argument, that's called a *counterclaim*. Let's reread this passage and look for the counterclaim in this argument." Her students soon locate it: *You might say that I am not mature enough to take care of a pet, but I have been keeping up with my grades, and you have let me do some short babysitting for my younger sister.* "That's it!" Ms. Miller says. "You've got it. Label that part the counterclaim. Next, we're going to build an argument together from the list you made using these same three elements: *claim, evidence,* and *counterclaim.* Which one shall we try together?"

Lectures

When it is necessary to build initial knowledge about a topic, a lecture is often the chosen format. A good lecture stimulates learners' curiosity and provokes critical thinking. It may *explain*, but it never just *tells*. Simply regurgitating information students could have read doesn't constitute a good lecture.

Almost everyone has had the misfortune of being on the receiving end of a bad lecture. Perhaps the speaker was not organized, meaning the flow of information was illogical and confusing. Maybe the speaker was indifferent to the needs of the audience and didn't pause to solicit questions, prompt dialogue, or allow time for reflection. Maybe the lecture incorporated offensive, biased language that alienated the audience. Or maybe the lecture was just boring—not because it lacked the razzle-dazzle of a stage show, but because the content was either something the audience already knew or so distant from the audience's prior knowledge that there was no bridge to understanding it, no way to get a toehold for cognitive engagement.

But what makes for a good lecture? The quick answer is accessibility and interactivity. By *accessibility,* we mean that the content must be relevant to students, understandable to them, and designed to build on existing knowledge while stretching them to consider new ideas. Additionally, the lecture's pacing and length must be developmentally appropriate and crafted with the specific audience of students in mind. This means that the language used is socially equitable and inclusive of them. The *interactivity* requirement is equally important. It means the lecture is designed in a way that is considerate of the audience's needs to ask questions, take notes, and reflect on what's presented. One of the innovations kicked off by widespread shifts to distance learning has been recording short videos of lectures embedded with intermittent questions that pause the video until the viewer supplies an answer. This practice allows students to view the lecture asynchronously, freeing up synchronous time to promote more guided and collaborative instruction. The evidence on the usefulness of interactive videos is strong, with an effect size of 0.54 (www.visiblelearningmetax.com). You can see in Figure 2.1 a summary of the qualities that students and educators say they value most in a lecture.

Figure 2.1	Characteristics of Effective Lectures
Characteristic	**The Lecturer...**
Social Equity	• Uses inclusive examples • Uses nonbiased language
Presentation Skills	• Is knowledgeable, current, and accurate in the subject • Uses examples that are relevant and meaningful to students • Is verbally fluent, with good public speaking skills
Motivation	• Arouses a sense of curiosity among students • Stimulates student interest • Presents the material in interesting ways
Modeling	• Shows enthusiasm for the subject and the students • Is an academic role model
Mode of Lecture	• Paces the lecture to allow students to take notes • Provide summaries throughout the lecture
Critical Thinking	• Encourages independence in learning • Challenges students' views of the world to stimulate critical reasoning
Cognitive Processes	• Has a clear structure to the lecture • Builds on students' prior and background knowledge • Pauses so that students can consolidate their thinking

Source: Fisher et al. (1998).

Assessment During Focused Instruction

Assessment cannot be left to the end of the lesson or the end of the week. During focused instruction, good teachers are noticing students' responses and reactions and looking for misconceptions so that they can make adjustments, moment by moment, to boost understanding.

Noticing

Noticing is fundamental to teaching, so much so that the relative ability of a teacher to engage in this practice is an important way of distinguishing novice teachers from expert ones (Donovan & Bransford, 2005). In fact, we would argue that noticing is a definitive behavior in teaching. After all, any number of curriculum materials—textbooks, videos—can present information. They can easily be structured to include a clear purpose and excellent modeling or demonstrations. But curricula do not notice what students do with the new learning or make rapid decisions about what should occur next; expert teachers can do that.

Expert teachers recognize that noticing and interpreting their students' thinking reveals the relative effectiveness of prior instruction and informs their subsequent instructional decisions. Novice teachers tend to use a too-simplistic measure that confuses noticing with evaluating: *Is the student right or wrong?* Evaluation, especially in these broad terms, is problematic because it can lead a teacher to reduce task complexity (so that it's not too hard to "get") rather than provide scaffolding to help students rise to the challenge. Choppin (2011) studied the practices of novice and expert middle and high school mathematics teachers to determine how their noticing practices affected subsequent teaching. In every case, the novice teachers reduced the complexity of the task by "narrowing the choices available for students and by minimizing opportunities for students to make connections by explaining their strategies and reflecting on other students' strategies" (p. 189). They justified their decisions by asserting that students just didn't get it. The expert teachers, on the other hand, "engaged students in mathematical communication, in terms of explaining their thinking and in terms of attending to other students' thinking" (p. 195). In one case, a teacher pressed for explanation and justification 18 times in a 30-minute period of whole-class instruction.

It is this teacher behavior that serves as the transition to guided instruction. You are observing, listening, and using your knowledge of the content, of novice learners, and of their likely misconceptions or partial understandings to help you formulate the questions, prompts, and cues you'll need to scaffold student learning during guided instruction.

Here's an example. In her geometry class, Tina Nguyen establishes the purpose of the lesson, which centers on measuring exterior angles of triangles. She also explains her language goal (to incorporate vocabulary into discussions and proofs) and social goal (to collaborate with peers in a group project). Before asking students to work in groups and solve problems and proofs, Ms. Nguyen models the process and pairs it with her mathematical thinking. She reads the definition of the theorem: "The measure of an exterior angle of a triangle is equal to the sum of the measures of the two nonadjacent interior angles." She then explains her understanding of the theorem:

> I know that *sum* is "to add up." It's the answer when we add something up. I also know that *nonadjacent* means "not next to"; *non* means "not" and *adjacent* means "next to" or "near." So this theorem is saying to me that the measure of the exterior angle—this one [she points to an exterior angle]—is equal to the sum of the two that are not directly next to the exterior angle I'm trying to figure out. I also know that some people call the nonadjacent angles remote interior angles, but that doesn't really help me here.

Next, Ms. Nguyen looks at a problem: "In *PQR*, $\angle Q = 45°$, and $\angle R = 72°$. Find the measure of an exterior angle at *P*." Again, she shares her thinking through direct explanation:

OK, so I know that one angle is 45° and the other one is 72°. Wait, I don't have to do this in my head. It is always helpful to draw a diagram and label it with the given information. Let's see, I'll label the triangle with the degree angles, like this, and see if it helps. Yes, it does. Now I can see which are nonadjacent angles and which I need to solve. Easy! Now it's just a calculation problem. I'm ready for another.

Ms. Nguyen continues this way through two more examples and then invites students to try solving another problem, using the small whiteboards on their desks. As they work, she watches for patterns to see where students are experiencing difficulty or success. She asks them to explain their solutions to a partner and listens to their discussions. In particular, Ms. Nguyen is listening for evidence that students are making connections to previously taught content. She is watching to see which students are using mathematical models to justify their answers. Most important, she is interpreting what she is seeing and hearing so she can decide whether to remain in the focused instruction phase or to move fully into guided instruction. She isn't evaluating or simply assembling a catalog of how many correct and incorrect solutions she sees. Rather, she is interpreting students' responses so that she will be able to further scaffold their understanding through appropriate questions, cues, and prompts (guided instruction).

As it happens, the students generate quite a few incorrect answers. A novice teacher might be tempted to scale back the complexity of the next problem, but Ms. Nguyen, an expert teacher, knows that student thinking is essential to learning complex material, and she knows that her role is to move them from informal to formal reasoning.

"We hung with this problem for at least 10 minutes," she noted afterward. "What's interesting is that, over that period of time, I began to hear my own modeling and thinking aloud being enacted by them. Giving them that language and insight into how I think really pays off when I see them beginning to apply similar rationales to explain their own thinking."

Misconception Analysis

The National Research Council's meta-analysis of practices that make a difference in history, mathematics, and science instruction for secondary students yielded three main recommendations:

- Teachers must know and anticipate misconceptions students possess about the concepts being taught.
- Educators must teach for factual knowledge in a systematic way.
- Students must be taught to be metacognitively aware of their learning (Donovan & Bransford, 2005).

There is a rich research record supporting how important it is for teachers to anticipate student misconceptions (e.g., Guzzetti et al., 1993). For example, young children may believe that multiplication always yields a larger number and, thus, become confounded when faced with multiplying fractions. Science students may hold the misconception that Earth is at the center of the universe, or they may confuse acceleration and speed. A teacher who has anticipated misconceptions can plan to address them during focused instruction—by using math manipulatives to show what occurs with fractions, for example, or by demonstrating a series of experiments on a skateboard to highlight the difference between speed and acceleration. Of course, not all misconceptions can be anticipated; they may only surface when the teacher has a chance to hear students' reasoning.

Consider this scenario: Robert Sanchez, who has been working with his science class on the concept of volume, has asked students to explain what they see as he performs a series of demonstrations. First, he says, he'd like them to create a working definition of *volume*. A moment later, he is recording their explanation: "Volume is the amount of space something takes up." Mr. Sanchez then places a heavy block in a pan of water filled to the top and asks the students to discuss what they see (some water spilled over the edge) and why they think this happened. Their discussion is on target, as all of them are able to describe the displacement effect. Mr. Sanchez then asks how they would measure the volume of the block. Antonio responds immediately: "You have to multiply! Multiply its length times width times height!" The other students nod in agreement, and soon they have calculated the volume of the block.

Next, Mr. Sanchez asks the group to predict what will occur when he repeats the experiment with objects of varying size, all irregularly shaped. Again, they are able to explain how each object displaces a different amount of water because each object takes up a different amount of space. Then he holds up an actual irregular object—a paperweight shaped like the school's lion mascot—and asks them how to calculate its volume. The group falls quiet.

Mr. Sanchez: OK, let's think about it for a moment. What do you know so far?

Claudia: That when you drop that in the water, the water has to go somewhere, and it gets pushed out of the pan.

Maureen: We know how to do the math for volume. We multiply the width and the length and the height.

Antonio: I think we need to measure the lion, just like we did with the block.

Mr. Sanchez hadn't expected this; he had thought the students would surmise that measuring the amount of water displaced when he dropped the paperweight in the pan would give them the information they needed. But he allows them to wrestle with this problem for several minutes, hoping that they will conclude on their own that their methodology is flawed. As they do, he asks questions from time to time, scaffolding their understanding of the problem they created for themselves. However, when they appear to be stymied despite his attempts to scaffold their thinking, he returns to another demonstration, this time thinking aloud about how he is solving the problem of calculating the volume of the object by noting the water level before and after the displacement effect.

Building Confidence and Competence Through Focused Instruction

Students with strong self-regulation know where they are in the learning journey and have confidence to take on the challenge of learning more. When teachers are clear about what students need to learn, they can support students' developing regulation. When students do not know what they are supposed to be learning, or what success looks like, they may be compliant and complete tasks, but they are less likely to accept the learning challenge.

As students participate in cognitive apprenticeship experiences during focused instruction, they begin to believe that they can do what they see their teachers doing. Much like in days gone by, when the apprentice watched the expert cobbler and slowly assumed responsibility for different aspects of shoemaking, students whose teachers practice modeling, demonstrations, direct instruction, and effective lectures can provide students with understandable introductions to concepts, skills, and strategies, setting them up to use these in the future to accomplish things that are important and relevant. The success built on this solid foundation is empowering, shaping students' sense of themselves as someone who writes and reads, thinks through problems, has questions, negotiates meaning, and so on.

Conclusion

There are many ways to establish purpose, model thinking, demonstrate skills, and notice student thinking; we have covered only a few. During the focused instructional phase of the gradual release of responsibility model, concepts and skills are introduced to students through a series of instructional moves that begins with establishing the purpose. To promote metacognition, the teacher can enhance cognitive apprenticeship experiences through think-alouds so that students can witness the thinking processes used to understand the concept or master the skill. As part of this phase, the teacher engages in noticing in order to interpret student reasoning and to listen for misconceptions. Collectively, these instructional moves define the learning target for the student and increase the likelihood of learning success.

3

Guided Instruction:
Questions, Prompts, and Cues

The guided instruction phase of the gradual release of responsibility instructional framework is the point where the cognitive load begins to shift from teacher to student. In guided instruction, the teacher follows the lead of the learners, who are challenged to apply a concept, skill, or strategy in a new situation. It's not unlike teaching a child to ride a bicycle—specifically, the stage when you are running alongside the novice rider, reaching out to steady them when they begin to wobble, and then letting go again after they have regained control. Knowing when to offer a steadying hand and when to withdraw it is truly the art and science of teaching.

Unlike teaching an individual child to ride a bike, teachers are orchestrating learning for large groups of students—focusing on scaffolding and developing skill or knowledge through questioning, prompting, and cuing. Sometimes, teachers work with the whole class; sometimes, they work with intentionally selected subgroups of students; and sometimes, yes, they do work with students one on one.

It's important to note that guided instruction conducted with small groups is not the same thing as ability grouping. *Ability grouping,* a permanent structure in which specific students are grouped with peers based on perceived ability, is an ineffective approach to increasing student performance and can be damaging to students' self-efficacy. Guided instruction, by contrast, is temporary, flexible, and responsive. There isn't a standard script to follow during guided instruction. The teacher's actions are predicated on what the students say and do, and what students' words and actions might reveal about their needs. For the teacher, this means maintaining a heightened sense of awareness and keeping up a stream of internal questions:

Does this student need a bit of reteaching before he is able to explain the differences between meiosis and mitosis? Is this group now ready to analyze a political cartoon critical of FDR's first 100 days in office because they understand the controversies of the time regarding government interference? Do I expect some students to have difficulty recognizing a scalene triangle when it is shown in a different orientation?

In other words, small-group guided instruction is not the same for every group, nor does it need to happen every day for every student. It's not likely that you will meet with every group on a daily basis, especially if you're teaching at the secondary level. Instead, you might meet with each group one to three times a week, depending on the length of the lessons. Some students need more guided instruction than others, so you will want to stack the deck a bit to meet with some groups more frequently. You also can alter the size of the groups, so that students who need more help are in groups with fewer members; this allows you more "face time" with them. Remember, though, that guided instruction should not be reserved for students who are struggling; those who perform at grade level but could be performing higher, as well as students who are advanced and need to be challenged, also deserve this type of targeted instruction and benefit from it. In a distance or blended learning environment, guided instruction occurs during synchronous time, while other students may be in breakout rooms or working asynchronously.

Scaffolding Students' Understanding

A hallmark of guided instruction is that the teacher–student dialogue is carefully crafted to move students toward understanding by following the principles of *scaffolding*. This term was coined as a metaphor for describing the temporary supports, in the form of questions, prompts, and cues, a teacher offers learners as a bridge toward a skill or concept they cannot otherwise perform or grasp independently (Wood et al., 1976). The smart scaffolding teachers intentionally undertake during guided instruction focuses on addressing student errors and misconceptions rather than on correcting students' mistakes.

The Difference Between Mistakes and Errors

When a student inaccurately interprets something due to inattention to the task (e.g., forgets an important step), that student is making a mistake, not an error. You know you're dealing with a mistake when you can give corrective feedback and immediately see the proverbial light bulb go on. Once corrected, students realize what they need to do next; they just need the time and space to do it.

Errors are more serious and require a more complicated response. Errors are what you're dealing with when you give students corrective feedback about a task or about the processes they need to deploy and get a blank stare in return. They simply don't know what you're talking about. Their lack of knowledge or misconceptions mean that your corrective feedback isn't enough to get their learning on track. These students need a return to focused instruction or additional guided instruction, and you need to adjust your plans accordingly.

Errors fall into four broad categories. Classifying them in this way can help to make instructional responses more precise and effective:

- *Factual errors* interfere with a student's ability to perform with accuracy. Life sciences teacher Kenya Jackson sees this with her students who have difficulty clarifying the differences and similarities between recessive and dominant traits. Students may not understand what constitutes a dominant trait, or they may incorrectly define certain terms.
- *Procedural errors* make it difficult to apply factual information. "When I teach how to use a Punnett square to predict probability about genotype," noted Ms. Jackson, "students can tell me what dominant and recessive alleles are, but they can't calculate them in a meaningful way." Students may fail to divide the two alleles correctly for each parent or to follow the procedure for matching alleles.
- *Transformation errors* occur when students incorrectly apply information to a new situation. Ms. Jackson noted that the Punnett square procedure is only valid when the traits are independent of one another. "Although I use examples and nonexamples in my teaching [that is, showing students right and wrong ways to do something], some of them still overgeneralize the procedure and try to use it with polygenic traits, such as hair color," she said. "For some, they've learned a tool, and now they want to use it in every situation."
- *Misconception errors* can result from the teaching itself. "I have to stay on guard for this," Ms. Jackson said. "Because I teach them Punnett squares, many students hold this misconception that one gene is always responsible for

one trait. These can be stubbornly held, so I have to teach directly with misconceptions in mind."

Track Errors and Find Error Patterns

Most of us have had the experience of stopping the class during a task because we have detected a pattern in the questions coming from students. When the fourth student in as many minutes asks the same question about the directions, it's a neon sign that the whole class would benefit from clarification.

Unfortunately, it's rare for a teacher to get so clear a signal. Elementary teachers spend six or seven hours a day in the company of their students, and it can be very difficult to recall who needed more help with multiplying fractions when they are also responsible for teaching language arts, science, and social studies. Secondary teachers have the opposite problem. Although the scope of their content teaching is more limited, they are seeing 150 or more students a day. Who can keep track?

One solution is to use a simple error analysis sheet (see Figure 3.1) to record all the information coming in. After identifying the major skills or concepts that have been taught, teachers can jot down the initials of the students who are making errors and, thus, require further instruction in the identified areas.

Distinguish Between Targeted and Global Errors

Using an error analysis sheet helps a teacher discover what kinds of instructional adjustments need to be made. In the case of the draft essay in Figure 3.1, for example, it's easy to see precisely who needs to receive small-group guided instruction. In other cases, a teacher might notice that one of the cells on the form is filling up with initials, which signals that some whole-group instruction addressing these specific skills or concepts would be beneficial. This kind of global error might show up within a single class period of students or extend to students in several periods.

Either way, it signals the need to reexamine the overall instructional design to figure out why the original plan didn't work—or didn't work in particular classes.

Figure 3.1	**Error Analysis Sheet**				
Date: __10/12__ Topic: __"What Sustains Us?" draft essay; focus on mechanics__					
Error	**Period 1**	**Period 2**	**Period 3**	**Period 4**	**Period 5**
Mid-sentence capitalization	JC			AA	
Colons and semicolons	JC, JT, AG, DL, TV	EC, MV, WK		AA, SK, MG, EM, BA, TS	HH, DP, MR, CH
Ending punctuation	JC, AG, SL	WK, MW		AA, BA	MR
Subject–verb	JC, JT, DL, MM, SL, ST, ND	RT, VE, VD, CC		AA, MG, SC, PM, LG	DP, DE
Tense consistency	DS	SJ, JM		AA, TR, PC	DE

Tracking errors is important because it prevents us from reteaching the entire class because we can't recall who needed help. When a large number of students across periods don't make progress, error analysis prevents us from sticking with a flawed instructional plan and may suggest a need to redesign the overall unit of study.

The Process and Tools of Guided Instruction

Once errors have been identified, it's time to get down to the work of using scaffolds to move students' learning

Try thinking of the guided instruction process in terms of a flowchart (see Figure 3.2). When one scaffold does not work, move on to the next. When the scaffold works, return to questioning to check for understanding or to probe deeper about students' knowledge. Let's take a closer look now at the three major types of scaffolds.

Questions

A basic assumption of guided instruction is that the students are responding in a logical manner given what they know and don't know at that particular moment. Therefore, the internal question a teacher should ask during this phase of instruction is this: *What does this student's answer tell me about what he knows and doesn't know?* Questions that check for understanding are very important during guided instruction, but questions that uncover errors and misconceptions are essential.

Asking students to elaborate or to clarify their answers allows you to determine how to respond and how best to scaffold understanding. For instance, when you hear a student read *horse* instead of *house,* you might flash on various explanations as to why:

- The student may not be attending closely to the word.
- The student may not yet be attending to the medial position in the word.
- The student may not be familiar with the vowel combination in the word.

That rapid hypothesis formulation must now be followed by a teacher response. For example:

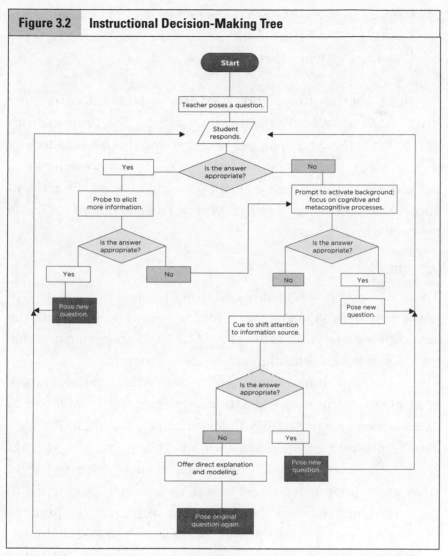

Figure 3.2   Instructional Decision-Making Tree

From "Identifying Instructional Moves During Guided Learning," by N. Frey and D. Fisher, 2010, *The Reading Teacher, 64*(2), p. 13. Copyright 2010 by John Wiley and Sons. Used with permission.

- *If you think the student is not attending to print:* "Look at the word again. Can you read it for me?"
- *If you think the student is having difficulty with medial positions:* "You missed the middle sound. Look again at the middle letters and try reading it again."

- *If you think the student is unfamiliar with the vowel combination:* "The letters *o* and *u* make the /*ow*/ sound. Try the word again using that sound."

The alternative to scaffolding, of course, is simple correction: "That word is *house*. Read it again, please." The problem with correction is that you don't get to test your hypothesis as to why the error was made. Scaffolding with prompts and cues gives you the chance to gain a better understanding of what the student knows and doesn't know so that you can take action to get learning back on track.

Prompts

There are a number of different things a teacher can say to engage learners in cognitive or metacognitive work. That's the key to giving a prompt: getting students to do some thinking. Figure 3.3 summarizes the different types of prompts.

Essentially, prompts are hints or reminders that encourage students to do the work when they have temporarily forgotten to use a known skill or strategy in an unfamiliar situation. Prompts can be phrased as statements or questions, but the teacher should not assume so much responsibility as to tell the student what information is missing. Instead, the prompt is designed to guide students' thinking. Over time, and with practice, students will begin to incorporate this type of thinking into their habits.

Here's a look at how prompting works. Ahmad Tarmizi is meeting with a group of students who generally perform at grade level but are not making much progress toward the mastery of the English language arts standard "Gather relevant information from multiple print and digital sources, assess the credibility and accuracy of each source, and integrate the information while avoiding plagiarism." As part of their conversation, Mr. Tarmizi uses prompts to guide his students' understanding:

Figure 3.3	Prompt Types and Examples	
Type of Prompt	**Definition**	**Examples**
Background knowledge	Reference to content that the student already knows, has been taught, or has experienced but has temporarily forgotten or is not using correctly	• *When a student is trying to solve a right-triangle problem:* "I'm thinking about the total degrees inside a triangle." • *During a science unit about the water cycle:* "What do you remember about states of matter?"
Process or procedure	A reminder of established or generally agreed-upon rules or guidelines that have been forgotten or are not being followed	• *When a student is pronouncing a word incorrectly:* "When two vowels go walking…" • *When a student gets the wrong answer from not following the order of operations:* "I'm thinking about a mnemonic that we use to remember the order for solving problems." • *When a student using a band saw accidentally breaks a board in two:* "Think about the role of the wood's grain. Remember the rule for that?"
Reflective	A reminder to students to be metacognitive and think about their thinking for the purpose of determining the next steps or the solution to a problem	• *When a student has just read something incorrectly:* "Does that make sense? Really think about it." • *When a student's writing does not include evidence, as the assignment required:* "What are we learning today? What was our purpose?"

Mr. Tarmizi: Which of these sources did your group rate as "credible and accurate"?

Dewa: All of them. They're all accurate. They all have statistics and information in them.

Ramzy: Yeah, they're credible, too.

Mr. Tarmizi: Why? I'm not saying that you're wrong; I just want to know how you reached that agreement. (questioning prompt)

Miguel: Well, because... I don't really know... they're all about the same topic.

Mr. Tarmizi: I'm thinking about the credibility tool we used a few weeks ago. There were items on that checklist.... (procedural prompt)

Dewa: Oh, yeah, look. They all have a copyright year!

Miguel: And there is a way to contact the author or publisher. So we could check that.

Mr. Tarmizi: Nice. Well done. Those are two important considerations. But also think about the author and what you know about the author. (background knowledge prompt)

Ramzy: We did that. We looked up the authors, and they have written other stuff about these topics. So I do think that they are credible. They seem like subject matter experts—is that what it was called?

Cues

Sometimes prompts are not sufficient, or there isn't a clear way to prompt the student. In these cases, what's called for is a cue. *Cues* shift the learner's attention. They are also more specific and direct than prompts, meaning the teacher bears more cognitive responsibility. We liken cuing to the sports commentator who uses instant replay and slow motion to get us to notice a particular technique: "Hey, look here! And look carefully." Figure 3.4 provides an overview of the different types of cues.

Cues are a common feature of teaching, especially during whole-class instruction and the initial introduction of content. Within the gradual release of responsibility instructional framework, they play an essential role when students are struggling. Rather than simply tell students the answer or how to apply the learning, the teacher uses cues to make sure students are taking on responsibility and doing the work.

Figure 3.4	Cue Types and Examples	
Type of Cue	**Definition**	**Examples**
Visual	A range of graphic hints to guide students' thinking or understanding	• Highlighting areas within text where students have made errors • Creating a graphic organizer to arrange content visually • Asking students to take a second look at a graphic or visual from a textbook
Verbal	Variations in speech to draw attention to something specific or verbal "attention getters" that focus students' thinking	• "This is important…" • "This is the tricky part. Be careful and be sure to…" • Repeating a student's statement using a questioning intonation • Changing voice volume or speed for emphasis
Gestural	Body movements or motions to draw attention to something that has been missed	• Pointing to the word wall when a student is searching for the right word or the spelling of a word • Making a predetermined hand motion • Placing thumbs around a key idea in a text that the student is missing

For example, when the students in Kelly McKee's class study World War I, she creates a number of language charts, a visual timeline, and a word wall so that students will have a number of cues readily available. As part of the lesson activities, students create graphic organizers of the content, including locations of the war, the people and countries involved, and the key terminology. When a group gets stuck with a review question, Ms. McKee can point them to the visual timeline, which helps them figure out their response. When another group has difficulty comparing the two world wars, she can direct them back to their graphic organizers and all the thinking about the content they have captured there.

Direct Explanations

When prompts and cues are not enough to resolve the errors and misconceptions that students have, the teacher needs to provide a direct explanation to resolve lingering confusion. This doesn't mean just correcting students and telling them the information that they missed; rather, it's a matter of shifting guided instruction back into focused instruction. The teacher reestablishes the learning purpose, provides an explanation with modeling and think-alouds, and then asks questions or sets small challenges in order to monitor student understanding:

- "Can you now explain the idea to your partner?"
- "Can you tell me what I just said in your own words?"
- "I'm going to ask you the original question again, now that you know _____."
- "How about writing a short summary of this in your notebook so you'll remember?"

Of course, students may not fully grasp the content at this point and may need additional guided instruction to really master the information, but right now, with prompts and cues having failed to clear up student confusion, the teacher is working toward a more modest goal: allowing students to experience some success. Think of it this way: If you do not understand something, despite significant efforts on the part of another person, at some point you will begin to doubt *yourself,* not the person providing the instruction. You might even think of yourself as stupid, at least in this one particular area. Many of the students we meet who believe they are "not good" at math, reading, writing, and so on are victims of this kind of debilitating negative thinking. Just that little bit of productive success they can achieve with appropriate scaffolding is often enough to reestablish a more positive learning outlook.

Guided Instruction in the Classroom

The major moves of guided instruction—questions, prompts, and cues—are useful in transferring responsibility to students while still providing appropriate scaffolds for learning. Now, we'll examine some of the different ways that teachers can integrate guided instruction into the classroom.

Guided Reading Instruction

While most of her kindergarten class works in collaborative groups or independently, teacher Darla Cotton calls five of her students to the reading table to read from the emerging-reader book *Wait for Me* by Michèle Dufresne, a decodable text that focuses on long *a* sounds and features dogs. Ms. Cotton has previously focused her instruction on left-to-right directionality, C-V-C words, and basic sight words. Now it's time for this group of students to apply these skills and strategies with unfamiliar text.

She directs individual children to begin "whisper reading," staggering start times so that they do not fall into a choral reading of the text. Ms. Cotton moves around the table, listening to each student read, pausing to ask questions or offer prompts when they encounter difficulty, and making anecdotal notes. She notices that the children have done well with moving across each page and have correctly used the pattern of the text.

After they finish, she asks them to retell what occurred in the story so that she can determine their comprehension. One student, David, stumbles in his retelling, so Ms. Cotton invites him to use the book to recall. She then asks about the last page— who are they waiting for? A minute or two of discussion among the children, with prompts from Ms. Cotton, and the group has arrived at a decision: they are waiting for Daisy. Satisfied that this group is progressing in using their emergent knowledge of phonics, sight words, concepts about print, and comprehension, she sends them back to their collaborative learning groups and reviews the notes she has taken. She will use what she has learned to develop the next lesson.

High school English teacher Matt Tangaroa has introduced the paradox as a literary device used by writers and storytellers throughout the world. He presented several statements for his focused instruction to model his thinking when encountering a statement that seems to contradict itself yet somehow reveals a deeper truth (such as "being cruel to be kind" or George Bernard Shaw's comment that "youth is wasted on the young"). He also demonstrated how he uses inferencing in order to unearth the unstated truth.

Now Mr. Tangaroa wants students to examine paradox in the context of poetry. He sits down with a group of six high school students and shows them a copy of a very short poem by John Donne (1572–1631):

> I am unable, yonder beggar cries, To stand, or move; if he say
> true, he lies.

Mr. Tangaroa formed this group of students based on assessment evidence showing they had difficulty making the kinds of inferences necessary to understand a paradox in complex literature. In advance of his guided instruction, he asked students to asynchronously review his previously recorded modeling lesson about paradox. During live instruction, he asks them each to read the poem aloud and then has them discuss in pairs the poem's meaning and why the author would say that the beggar was a liar. Through prompts and cues, Mr. Tangaroa leads the six students to understand the unstated paradox. One of the students notes, "By speaking, the beggar was moving, and so he was lying."

Mr. Tangaroa later meets with another group of students—those his assessment data suggest are still confused by the basic concept of paradox and in need of additional instruction. Instead of referring these students to the recording of the prior modeled lesson, he thinks aloud about a new poem, Robert Frost's "Nothing Gold Can Stay." The first line's statement that "Nature's first green is gold" is a more accessible paradox for them consider, as it does not use Donne's antiquated syntax and refers to a phenomenon that he knows will be familiar to his students. After modeling his approach to the Frost poem, Mr. Tangaroa guides this group through several other accessible examples, building their skill and confidence, before finally asking them to unpack the paradox in the Donne poem.

Thanks to a clear learning target and assessment information, Mr. Tangaroa is able to use guided instruction to calibrate the scaffolding he provides and teach the same reading skills to a range of learners.

Guided Writing Instruction

During guided instruction, students apply what they have learned from focused instruction and collaborative learning, with varying degrees of support from the teacher. Teachers often use sentence or paragraph frames to scaffold students' academic writing. These frames, models, or templates help students internalize conventional structures.

Aida Allen uses paragraph frames to help her students internalize academic writing. As part of a unit of study on characters, Ms. Allen meets with a group of students who have been having difficulty with character summaries and analysis. She presents a paragraph frame (see Figure 3.5) to her students and asks them to read it aloud, adding information orally based on the different books they have been reading.

As Ms. Allen listens to her students, she provides additional, individualized cues and prompts as needed. For example, as Arturo suggests details about a character named Marty from

Phyllis Reynolds Naylor's *Shiloh,* Ms. Allen asks him to list words to describe Marty as he was at the beginning of the novel. Arturo says that Marty was shy and that he played by himself all the time. In response to her question about what else he remembers about Marty, Arturo shrugs. So Ms. Allen prompts him by saying, "Well, Marty was always looking around for things. What does that tell us about his personality?" Arturo and Ms. Allen agree that Marty was curious. Ms. Allen then turns her attention to Isabel, who isn't sure what her character, Esperanza from Pam Muñoz Ryan's *Esperanza Rising,* had learned. After the group completes the task of reading the paragraph frame aloud and adding details from their books, Ms. Allen asks them to use the frame to construct a paragraph in their journals. Here's what Arturo writes:

> Marty is one of the characters in the story. He is 8 years old and lives with his family in a house in the country. At the beginning of the story, Marty is a curious but shy boy who likes to play by himself. Marty faces a problem when he finds a stray dog. He knows who the dog belongs to and does not want to return him. He attempts to solve the problem by lying to his family and friends, but then he is caught. Finally, he is able to solve the problem by working hard and treating the dog's owner with respect. At the end of the story, he has learned that if you are honest and treat others with respect, then people will respect you.

Guided writing and the use of frames, models, and templates are not limited to the elementary school classroom. College composition experts Gerald Graff and Cathy Birkenstein (2009) recommend the use of frames (they call them templates) as an effective way for developing students' academic writing skills:

> After all, even the most creative forms of expression depend on established patterns and structures. Most songwriters, for

instance, rely on a time-honored verse-chorus-verse pattern, and few people would call Shakespeare uncreative because he didn't invent the sonnet or dramatic forms that he used to such dazzling effect.... Ultimately, then, creativity and originality lie not in the avoidance of established forms, but in the imaginative use of them. (pp. 10–11)

Figure 3.5   Character Analysis Paragraph Frame

_____ is one of the characters in the story. _____ is _____ and lives _____ (With whom? Where?). At the beginning of the story, _____ is _____ but _____ who _____ . _____ faces a problem when _____

_____ .

_____

_____ attempts to solve the problem by _____

_____

but _____ .

Finally, _____ is able to solve the problem by _____

_____

At the end of the story, _____ has learned that _____ if _____ , then _____

_____ .

Guided Instruction with Student Think-Alouds

Think-alouds are commonly thought of as a teacher-directed instructional practice, as we discussed in Chapter 2. Indeed, a think-aloud is a powerful tool for making thinking transparent to a group of learners. However, the real goal of thinking aloud is to prepare students to surface their own thinking processes as they learn and understand a new concept.

Student think-alouds are conducted in much the same way as teacher think-alouds. As students read a piece of text or perform a task, they pause to explain their thinking, including decisions they are making about what to do next. Student think-alouds are ideally suited for guided instruction, as they provide an opportunity to listen to the thinking processes of your students as they engage in new learning.

Lauren McDonnell's 6th grade history students had been introduced to the Code of Hammurabi during her focused instruction. When Ms. McDonnell read their "ticket out the door" written summaries at the end of class, she noticed that several of her students had difficulty explaining the pros and cons of the laws of ancient Babylon. She decided to meet with this group to review excerpts from their textbook, asking them to think aloud as they read. She hoped that by doing this she would gain insight into their reasoning.

Ms. McDonnell begins by distributing the text and quickly reviews the significance of this earliest preserved record of law, asking the students to think aloud about their impressions of fairness as they read. At Ms. McDonnell's request, Alex reads the portion of the code containing the *lex talionis,* better known as "an eye for an eye, a tooth for a tooth":

> *Ms. McDonnell:* Stop there, Alex, and tell me how you understand that term.
>
> *Alex:* Well, I guess I've got this picture in my head of a judge taking someone's eyeball out because the other guy lost his. Pretty gross.

Ms. McDonnell encourages Alex to read on and continue thinking aloud. Alex reads that the law only applies to injuries suffered by a free man, not enslaved people or children.

> *Alex:* I'm thinking that that doesn't seem very fair, like some people don't count. Girls and stuff. Shouldn't there be an "eye for an eye" rule for everyone?

Ms. McDonnell: What did you do there just now—when you were thinking aloud?

Alex: I asked myself a question about being fair.

Ms. McDonnell: Exactly! That's how you start to form opinions about pros and cons. Make a note about that on your T-chart. Ricardo, how about if you think aloud about the next section, about family laws?

The students continue in this fashion for the next 10 minutes, reading parts of the text and commenting aloud about their thought processes. At the end of the lesson, each student has some ideas noted for the pros and cons of the Code of Hammurabi, and they will be able to return to their collaborative learning groups to contribute to a project on the importance of these laws on civilization.

Guided Instruction Through Close Reading

Close reading is another form of guided instruction. It is often done with the whole class but also can be implemented with smaller groups of students. Close reading provides students an opportunity to try on some of the things that they have learned and practiced in other phases of the gradual release of responsibility instructional framework. The key features of close reading include the following:

- Focus on a complex, worthy text
- Repeated reading of the entire text and portions of the text
- Annotation of the text while reading, including underlining key ideas, circling words or phrases that are confusing, writing questions in the margins, and summarizing and synthesizing information in the margins
- Text-dependent questions that require students to produce evidence from the text as part of their responses and

- Extensive discussions among students about the text under investigation

During close readings of complex text, the teacher uses scaffolds but avoids front-loading or pre-teaching vocabulary. In other words, instead of relying on "front-end scaffolds," students use scaffolds distributed throughout the instruction in the form of questions, prompts, and cues. Some back-end scaffolds might also be provided for students who still need instruction following the close reading.

Let's look at an example. Ninth grade English teacher Dustin Bradshaw uses E. B. White's short story "Death of a Pig" to introduce his students to close reading. On their first reading of the text, which centers on the first five paragraphs, Mr. Bradshaw asks the students to focus on four questions and to use their annotation skills as they read:

- What is this passage mainly about?
- How is the passage organized?
- What words or phrases stand out to me as I read?
- Have I used structural and contextual analysis to resolve unknown words and phrases?

After reading the excerpt, the students, in their table groups, briefly discuss what they found. Mr. Bradshaw listens in on his students' conversations and is pleased to note that they generally understood the text and its organization.

Over the next several days, he asks students to reread the text and discuss their thinking about various text-dependent questions with their peers. Mr. Bradshaw developed significantly more text-dependent questions than he actually used. As he notes, "I keep a lot of different questions in my back pocket for when their conversations falter. I really want them to talk about all of these things, but sometimes a just-right question is needed to restart their thinking and talking." See Figure 3.6 for a list of his questions.

Figure 3.6	Sample Text-Dependent Questions for Close Reading

Text: E. B. White's "Death of a Pig"

General Understandings
- Who is the narrator? What is his job?
- What is the conflict presented in Section 1 of this essay?
- Who are the characters? Describe them.

Key Details
- Is the narrator sick?
- What is the end result of the "first degree"?
- What is the pig's reaction to the oil?
- What is the dog compared to in Section 2?
- What is the narrator's community like?
- In Section 2, how do we know the pig is sick?
- How is the pig buried? Why is this significant?

Structure
- What is the extended metaphor being set up? What is the purpose?
- Locate areas of personification. What is the effect?
- What is the time sequence of the essay?
- Locate areas where the tone of the essay shifts. What is the purpose for this shift?
- Locate areas of foreshadowing. What event is being hinted at?

Vocabulary
- How is the term *scheme* defined?
- What are the people on the farm referred to as? Why?
- How is the treatment of the pig defined?
- What is the pig referred to as?

Author's Purpose
- How does the narrator link his own experiences with that of the pig?
- Does the narrator care about his pig? For what reasons?
- In Section 3, what does the pig's death represent?
- How do the narrator's emotions change in Section 3?
- What makes the pig's burial more "decent" than a human one?

Inferences Across the Text
- How does the narrator's attitude toward the dog change throughout the text?
- What ties the pig and the narrator together?
- By the end of the text, how does the narrator feel about his original plan for the pig? Cite specific evidence to support your thinking.

At one point on the second day of the close reading, Mr. Bradshaw notes that students are not picking up on the author's use of personification. He reminds the class of this literary device, providing them with two examples, which he displays on the document camera:

> "*The house sighed with sadness.*" This communicates the idea that the house is gloomy looking, or not completely stable. And here's another: "*As he devoured the carcass, the vulture laughed with delight.*" I'd say the image of the vulture is enriched with the idea that it laughs in a sinister way. Including that phrase makes the vulture seem more evil than it might otherwise.

Mr. Bradshaw then asks the students to reread the text, considering the author's use of personification. They quickly get to work in their groups to find examples of personification:

> *Cindy:* In Section 2, he says, "In the upset position the corners of his mouth had been turned down, giving him a frowning expression." See, that is making us think that the pig has human characteristics.

> *Roel:* In the dog section it says, "Ours was a businesslike procession, with Fred, the dishonorable pallbearer, staggering along in the rear, his perverse bereavement showing in every seam in his face." I think that's what we're looking for, because really the dog could not be sad because of the pig dying.

Differentiation in Guided Instruction

As Tomlinson (2014) points out, a teacher can differentiate content, process, and product. The guided instruction phase of the gradual release of responsibility instructional framework allows for differentiation of all three components. Keep in mind that differentiation should always be in service of moving students upward on a staircase of complexity.

Content Differentiation

During small-group guided instruction, teachers can change the texts students are reading. They can change the mathematics problems students are expected to complete. They can vary the rate of learning expected or extend the content for some students beyond what others are learning, allowing for an enriched curriculum for those who have already mastered grade-level or course expectations. It is not assumed that the same students will always participate in accelerated learning or will need the text difficulty reduced; these instructional decisions are predicated on good assessment information. One way to ensure that the same students aren't grouped the same way for every unit is to include interest groups as part of guided instruction.

Process Differentiation

Differentiating process during guided instruction means adjusting activities. For example, teachers can vary the types of prompts used, based on student needs or strengths. They can vary the kinds of questions they ask or the level of support they provide. They can increase or decrease the visual support that is provided or encourage peer "language brokers" to talk with one another in their home language. Some students may benefit from encountering content via audiobooks, and others, from having content introduced to them before it is introduced to the large group so that they will have prior knowledge to draw upon. We have personally had great success offering "previews of coming attractions" in the form of graphic organizers or other visual displays so that learners possess a general schema in advance of the unit.

Product Differentiation

The products that students generate as part of guided instruction are the record of their developing skills and understanding and extremely valuable as assessment of students' learning. Teachers differentiate products in order to provide students with the best vehicle for showing what they know and can do. For some students, a conversation with the teacher does the trick. Others need to read and write. For still others, a performance or project might be the best approach.

The key to differentiating products is to create a menu of options. Teachers can choose which product they believe will best allow students to demonstrate mastery, or they can allow students to make that choice for themselves, with consultation and encouragement to stretch beyond their comfort zone. In the latter arrangement, a teacher might categorize product options according to type and then require each student to complete at least one from each category over the course of the semester:

- Oral language (e.g., meet with the teacher, teach a peer)
- Written language (e.g., write an essay, write a blog post, create a poem)
- Performance (e.g., deliver a public speech, write and perform a skit)
- Project (e.g., research a topic, create a visual representation or model)

When students choose a product to generate during guided instruction, they are grouping themselves according to that category, an interest group of sorts. It's just one of many ways that integrating the components of differentiated instruction and guided instruction allows us to be more responsive to each student's needs, strengths, and interests.

Assessment During Guided Instruction

As part of guided instruction, students are grouped and regrouped based on their performance, not on the teacher's perception of their ability. The most effective guided instruction is based on assessment information that is directly linked with content standards. For example, if the class is studying literary devices, the assessment data gathered might include a student's ability to recognize these devices and to use these devices when writing. Assessment results could be used to form groups based on identified needs (for example, one group that needs further instruction in the difference between foreshadowing and flash-back, and another group that needs additional instruction in using personification to humanize something not human).

As we have stated, it's critical to check for understanding and provide course correction (the steadying hand on the bicycle) as students begin to take on new concepts, skills, and strategies. Some of the ways that teachers might gather assessment data were covered in the examples earlier in the chapter, but let's augment those techniques with a few more.

Assessing Reading Instruction

In her guided instruction, kindergarten teacher Darla Cotton listens to her students read. In addition to providing prompts and cues, she compares their decoding skills with the most recent progress monitoring data she has from a more formal assessment. She also notes their fluency, both rate and prosody, to inform decisions about additional instruction her students will need. As noted earlier, this assessment allows her to group and regroup her students. Retellings are a useful way of measuring the extent to which a student has comprehended the reading. Retelling rubrics are included in many reading programs and are often a part of a district's bank of informal assessments. Teachers can use retelling inventories to plan guided instruction with the whole class or small groups.

Assessing Writing Instruction

Guided instruction in writing yields a permanent product, which serves as a great information source on students' status. Again, holistic or trait-specific rubrics are useful for analyzing writing. Students can use these rubrics to score their own writing (and the teacher can validate and challenge students' self-assessments). These rubrics help to build a learner's understanding of the expectations and measures of success that need to be internalized. Student self-scoring also increases metacognition, as learners are able to witness their gains over time.

Assessing Student Think-Alouds

Student think-alouds are a bit trickier to assess because the product—talking—is so ephemeral. The best way to get a snapshot of student understanding from a think-aloud is to prepare a checklist (see Figure 3.7) covering what you are listening for (the purpose, such as reading comprehension strategies or critical-thinking skills). As students think aloud, you can note the qualities that they exhibit and note, too, what they do not do. Over time, patterns may emerge, which you might use as a learning objective for future guided instruction. A distance learning innovation has been to have students record and submit 90-second think-alouds in advance for the teacher to assess.

Building Confidence and Competence Through Guided Instruction

It almost goes without saying, but when teachers guide students' thinking, students are expected to experience success. And success is motivating. Anyone who has experienced success wants to get that feeling back. As students engage with their teachers in these guided experiences, they begin to see that their efforts result in good things—specifically, learning and the feeling of success. This builds students' sense of agency and identity and increases their confidence.

In addition, guided instruction helps students develop habits that they can use to self-regulate their learning. In part,

Figure 3.7	Checklist for Assessing a Student Think-Aloud	
Student Name:		**Date:**
Comprehension	Did the student... ❑ Make connections to other texts? ❑ Visualize? ❑ Question the text? ❑ Make inferences beyond the text? ❑ Determine importance of information? ❑ Summarize?	Notes/examples:
Content knowledge	Did the student... ❑ Activate background knowledge? ❑ Use word derivations? ❑ Use context clues? ❑ Use resources? ❑ Apply new knowledge?	Notes/examples:
Evaluation	Did the student... ❑ Offer opinions? ❑ Speculate? ❑ Seek other sources? ❑ Notice omissions? ❑ Analyze arguments?	Notes/examples:

self-regulation requires that students monitor their progress. They note that they are making progress and it feels good. As students continue to interact with the teacher in guided learning, this aspect of self-regulation keeps developing, increasing their confidence.

But guided instruction does something else: it builds competence. Intentional scaffolded learning experiences are designed to close the gap between what a student already knows and what that student needs to know. As these gaps close, the student's proficiency increases. And as the student's proficiency increases and the student *recognizes* this gain, the student feels more confident about accepting the challenge of further learning.

Conclusion

Guided instruction serves as a linchpin between the focused instruction students have received and the independent learning they will need to complete.

The demand on the teacher is high during this phase, particularly because these lessons are subject to quick changes in direction, depending on where the learners lead you. Students are typically grouped with other learners who are similarly performing, based on assessment information, but the groupings change frequently as teachers and students monitor progress. The guided instruction phase can be used to differentiate instruction, as needed, by content, process, or product; the small group size allows for higher levels of customization. The goal of guided instruction is teaching that ultimately increases the rate of learning because students do not have to learn again what they already know or try to fill in knowledge gaps on their own. The art and science of teaching come together in this phase, as the teacher responds to the nuances of understanding each student exhibits.

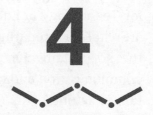

Collaborative Learning: Creating Student Learning Communities

In the collaborative learning phase of the gradual release of responsibility instructional framework, students are expected to apply the skills and knowledge they have been taught and to turn to one another for support and enrichment. As they interact, their learning moves forward, and they have the opportunity to use and develop critical soft skills like effective communication, leadership, and negotiation.

The Case for Collaborative Learning

Perhaps no element of the gradual release of responsibility instructional framework better captures the essence of college and career readiness than collaborative learning. Students' ability to communicate and collaborate is rightfully seen as crucial for success. The Partnership for 21st Century Skills (2009) calls for students to "exercise flexibility and willingness to be helpful in making necessary compromises to accomplish a common goal" (p. 4). ASCD's Whole Child (n.d.) approach's indicators of success for student engagement include opportunities for students to participate in inquiry, decision making, goal setting, self-monitoring, and time management. The International Society for Technology in Education (2012) states that "digital age skills are vital for preparing students to work, live, and contribute to the social and civic fabric of their communities" and defines communication and collaboration (both face-to-face and at a distance) as one of six major standards for student learning (para. 2). In an age where digital communication has become so critical to schooling, attention to the skills that support collaboration is warranted.

Teamwork, attitude, and the ability to network and solve problems are collectively referred to as *soft skills* and identified as key to employment opportunities. The U.S. Department of Labor Office of Disability Employment Policy (2012) states that "soft skills pay the bills" when it comes to workplace readiness and notes that they "cannot be taught in a vacuum... rather, they must be introduced, developed, refined, practiced, and reinforced" (p. 8). Finally, the National Association of Colleges and Employers (2012), an organization dedicated to connecting college students to internships and careers, notes that the soft skills employers most value include leadership, teamwork, verbal communication, and problem solving.

Clearly, problem-solving group skills are essential to college and career readiness, and this is a compelling argument for using collaborative learning. But as educators, we also need to pay attention to the "here and now," and that means ensuring our students acquire the academic knowledge of the disciplines we teach. A significant body of evidence suggests that, regardless of the subject matter or content area, students learn more and retain information longer when they work in small groups (www. visiblelearningmetax.com). Students who work in collaborative groups also appear more satisfied with their classes, complete more assignments, and generally like school better (Summers, 2006).

Collaborative learning is critical in developing the habits of mind necessary within various disciplines. Take science, for instance. It is popular for educators to promote "thinking like a scientist" as an overarching goal, but when instruction doesn't match this goal, such thinking is undermined. Science students often wrongly believe that the content of their textbooks is set in stone. They don't realize that scientific knowledge evolves precisely because scientists debate findings and engage in discourse meant to expose multiple interpretations (Osborne & Dillon, 2010). Although most of us do not grow up to be scientists in the formal sense, we interact daily with science as members of the public.

Collaborative learning tasks that are structured to provoke debate allow students to engage in true scientific thinking—and we aren't referring strictly to controversial topics in science. In many content areas, it's possible to challenge students to examine conflicting quantitative and qualitative data and ask them to draw conclusions and support their claims. That's thinking like a scientist.

Of course, collaborative learning isn't just a matter of designing a task, putting several students together, and then hoping for the best. The goal is to create student learning communities in which individuals encourage, extend, and expand on one another's thinking (Fisher et al., 2020).

Turning Student Collaboration into Student Learning Communities

Decades of research about professional learning communities (PLCs)—structures that are familiar to many teachers—provide guidance on how to maximize the benefits and expand the possibilities of student collaboration. As it happens, student learning communities require many of the same conditions adult learning communities do.

Provide Tasks and Experiences That Encourage Student Dialogue

The first condition has to do with the *experiences and the tasks* themselves. Tasks must be designed to prompt the kind of discussion that the group needs to cognitively engage. In other words, students need a reason and a path to make meaning *with* one another. In doing so, they employ both academic and social language.

For example, in language arts, they might be asked to compare two pieces of text in order to reconcile conflicting information about the same topic. The built-in dissonance of the clashing perspectives will fuel discussion. In science, they might pore over lab results after culturing bacteria from their own cheek swabs; the surprise and the struggle to make sense of the results will foster discussion. Or in social studies, they might be asked to determine what does and does not belong in a list of items a nomadic people would need to move their animals from one grazing area to the next. There, it's the process of debating and arriving at consensus that will spark discourse.

Create and Sustain Relationship Conditions That Empower Learning

A second condition involves *supportive relational conditions* needed for a group to work productively. Social cohesion—that is, the positive bonds among the members of the group—is crucial to their success.

One large study of nearly 2,000 middle school students found that learning with peers across races and ethnicities created positive gains in peer relatedness and reduced inequitable disparities to the point where the academic trajectory of students of color was the same as white students (Van Ryzin et al., 2020). Regular contact with others using principles of supportive peer learning made the difference. Instead of waiting for supportive relational conditions to be in place, it's up to the teacher to foster them by creating opportunities for students to regularly work together. Successful student learning communities emerge over time. They are not something that teachers can simply direct students to "do."

Establish Shared Agreements About Success

Too often in group learning, the tacit goal is simple task completion: *get it done.* Having a *shared agreement of group success* is a way to ensure that groups are moving toward a common goal of quality as well as completion. Always share the purpose for an activity and its specific learning targets, but make sure the value of learning in this collaborative way is clear to all by linking individual goals with group goals.

For example, asking students to rate their individual level of confidence in meeting the task's success criteria and then compare their ratings with those of others in their group signals to them that they each play a role in the success of the others. Give them time to discuss the success criteria and their confidence about meeting these criteria rather than just asking them to dive into the activity. The few extra minutes it takes up front can prevent the "ready, fire, aim" phenomenon of a group rushing to complete a task without really thinking it through—and without capitalizing on all its learning potential.

Promote Intentional Collective Learning

Teams need the time to engage in the *intentional collective learning* that comes from being able to debrief and reflect on their work. We're not referring here to the unfortunate practice of having students rate the other members of the group, which is a sure way to undermine relational trust. We mean asking students to consider their own performance in light of the results:

- What contributions did I make?
- What additional contributions could I have made?

- What is an example of when I worked well in our group?
- What is one thing that I could have done better?

This is an important yet often overlooked component of collaborative group work. Students in their groups need the chance to reflect individually, debrief collectively, and compare their results to the success criteria. This is how they calibrate their individual and collective efforts over time.

Encourage Students to Leverage Peer Supports to Amplify Learning

The fifth condition for student learning communities—the *leveraging of peer supports to amplify learning*—is, in many ways, a key aim of social-emotional learning. Students will learn more, more deeply and more expansively, if they know how to seek help from one another, communicate effectively, and give and receive feedback. Language frames can help to shape these skills, especially for younger learners; however, teachers must also model these themselves. A study of middle school mathematics classrooms found that students rarely exhibited these behaviors during team learning activities because their teachers rarely evidenced those behaviors themselves, despite stated norms (Webb et al., 2006).

Do you want your students to seek help and feel comfortable seeking help? Make sure they see you doing it. Do you want them to seek feedback and be comfortable using feedback to adjust their learning approaches and their interactions with others? Make sure you are doing so regularly.

Foster Leadership Skills

The sixth and final condition for student learning communities is ongoing *development of all students' leadership skills*. The civic engagement of a classroom community is a central feature of this approach. Teams come together to discuss their work while the teacher prompts them to consider ways they might tackle future conflicts and solve problems going forward.

Another way to foster leadership is to give student opportunities to expand their learning through their own exploration. Genius Hour is an example of how student teams can propose a project and learn about it through mostly self-directed inquiry. However, this isn't feasible or even necessary for all classrooms. More common is the rotating use of roles and responsibilities within group assignments so that students broaden their experiences beyond their comfort zone. Of course, no one benefits from being the notetaker every time the team takes on a new task. As students get to know one another and experience different roles, allow them to make internal decisions about how they will manage tasks.

Collaborative Learning's Common Features and Key Distinctions

Regardless of the task configuration, length of the experience, or degree of learning community currently achieved, all collaborative learning has three important features in common:

- It involves sustained interaction with at least one peer.
- The interaction includes what Resnick (1995) calls "accountable talk"—discussions guided by a set of agreements (e.g., we will stay on topic, we will embrace accuracy, we will think deeply about what our teammates say) and structured by conversational techniques (e.g., *this* is how we will ask for clarification and explanation, *this* is how we'll challenge misconceptions, *this* is how we'll build on our teammates' contributions).
- The discourse of the interaction is rooted in the lesson's academic language.

However, there is a real difference in the types of tasks students might engage in during collaborative learning. Some tasks are best described as *basic group work,* while other, results-oriented tasks fall into the category of *productive group work.* Both are useful in learning—neither is "better" or "more advanced" than the other; they just serve different purposes. The diagram in Figure 4.1 compares and contrasts these two forms of collaborative learning, which we'll take a closer look at now.

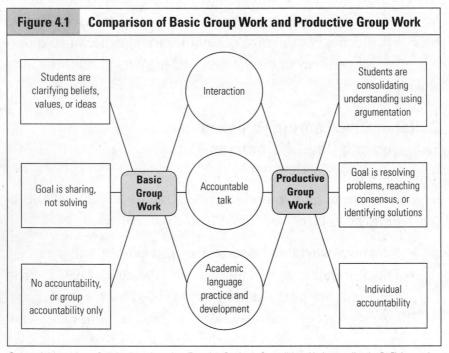

Figure 4.1   Comparison of Basic Group Work and Productive Group Work

Source: Adapted from *Collaborative Learning: Ensuring Students Consolidate Understanding,* by D. Fisher and N. Frey. Copyright 2012 by the International Reading Association. Used with permission.

Basic Group Work: For Sharing Information and Exchanging Ideas

In basic group work, the students share their own ideas, values, or beliefs and consider those of others. These sharing activities are the most common kind of group work we see. A good example is the classic "think-pair-share" arrangement and its many variations, such as think-write-pair-share and think-pair-square (where two pairs join together to extend their discussion), which we've seen used in nearly every classroom we've ever been in. These sharing tasks tend to be brief, and many are deployed on the fly for purposes of engagement and classroom management, especially when students indicate that their attention is beginning to wander.

Other kinds of basic group work are more extended and purposeful. For example, Art Hollingsworth, a Family and Human Services teacher in his district's Career and Technical Education pathway, uses *virtual opinion stations* to provoke discussion about beliefs and values in one of his units. Here's how he explains his approach:

> I teach about mandatory reporting requirements for the profession, but I'm also working with adolescents who have a very different set of beliefs about privacy. They value keeping secrets because they've learned that it's important in friendships. I need them to see that mandatory reporting of suspected abuse and neglect among clients is not the same as keeping a harmless secret between two friends.

Mr. Hollingsworth has labeled four breakout rooms: Strongly Agree, Agree, Disagree, and Strongly Disagree. ("I don't use Neutral, because I want to force them to take a stand," he told us.) After he reads aloud brief scenarios of Family and Human Services personnel being confronted with evidence of possible abuse or neglect and their decision on whether to report it to a state agency, students then choose the breakout room that best fits their opinion regarding the decision, and they discuss it with their peers. "One scenario in particular gets them stirred up," Mr. Hollingsworth said. "I give them a case of a childcare worker who repeatedly sees bruises on a child, with the mom explaining it away as a clumsy child." Many of his students want to debate the childcare worker's decision to file a report, claiming that she didn't have evidence. "This really pushes their thinking, and we go back into the language of the mandatory reporting law, which states that they don't need to investigate, only to suspect." His goal—for students to clarify their values and beliefs—paves the way for more instruction.

Another way to incorporate a planned exchange of ideas is to use a *carousel* arrangement, in which groups of students rotate through a series of stations, gathering information (often background knowledge) for the purpose of discussion. Third grade teacher Emily Aldrich uses a carousel as part of a science unit on the properties of light. Students visit a station that features a prism (so they can learn about refraction), another station focusing on shadows (to see how sources of light alter the shapes of the shadows), and a third featuring compact discs. In this last station, students experiment with locating different light sources (e.g., the natural light coming through the classroom windows) and tilting the CDs just so to find the rainbow reflection. At each station, they discuss and record their observations.

Ms. Aldrich told us how using the carousel arrangement supports her instructional goals:

> This is my introduction to a unit [on light], and I want them to grasp two concepts right away. The first is that I want them to notice that when you change the position of the light source relative to an object, the shadow it casts changes as well. The second is that visible light refracts into a rainbow of colors. Later, we'll be looking at how the reflection and absorption of visible light dictates the perceived color of an object. I'll use their observations as a springboard.

Ms. Aldrich's use of basic group work is an example of how collaborative learning can be used in an inquiry-based classroom. As we have noted, there is a misconception that the gradual release of responsibility instructional framework requires that every lesson proceed through a strict sequence, with collaborative learning always following focused or guided instruction. But many classrooms, especially science ones, regularly use inquiry to foster curiosity, activate background knowledge, and set the stage for new learning. By opening the unit with collaborative learning, Ms. Aldrich is tapping into the concepts, knowledge, and skills her students already possess as they write and discuss their observations. She is not introducing new knowledge; she is asking students to apply their existing knowledge to a novel situation. Her goal for her student learning community is consistent with the goals of basic group work, in that she wants her students to share ideas but not yet resolve problems or identify solutions. For that, she will choose a productive group work arrangement.

Productive Group Work: For Solving Problems and Finding Solutions

As noted, basic group work is valuable because it allows students to express their ideas, values, and beliefs, and it gives them an opportunity to apply listening and speaking skills as they engage with classmates. But basic group work primarily draws on existing knowledge.

A crucial aspect of the gradual release of responsibility instructional framework is that students encounter problems that require them to consolidate and advance their thinking, using newer knowledge in order to reach resolution. This goal is markedly different from those associated with basic group work, and it is the hallmark of productive group work. This type of group work is especially useful for fostering the development of the student learning community, as many of the conditions outlined in the previous section are needed for teams to be successful. In productive group work, there is always a product, accountability is at the group and the individual levels, and students use argumentation—especially furnishing evidence—to support their conclusions.

Solving problems and identifying solutions are central thinking goals in productive group work. This means students must apply the soft skills related to timekeeping, goal setting, and making work plans for the group. These can be especially challenging for young students, who will benefit from scaffolding—supports such as language frames that provide a structure for their discussions, note-taking sheets designed to capture the group's ideas, and checklists for tasks that require multiple meetings, such as those that involve research and presentation of ideas.

There are many well-known instructional routines teachers can utilize for productive group work. We have five favorites—techniques that are not discipline-specific and are easily transferable to varied subject matter. In fact, we encourage teachers who share students—co-teachers or members of a grade-level team, especially—to teach these five routines so that they can be easily enacted across content areas.

Discussion Roundtable

We were inspired by the work of English teacher and author Jim Burke (2002) to adapt the technique he calls *conversational roundtable* to promote discussion and note taking within productive work groups. We ask students to fold a sheet of paper into fourths and then fold down the interior corner in order to create a diamond in the center of the opened page (see Figure 4.2). Students make their own notes in the upper left quadrant of the graphic organizer and then explain their thinking to the rest of the group. Members of the group record notes about one another's ideas and then write a summary or conclusion in the center. The group submits their graphic organizers to the teacher, who now has a record of how the conversation evolved, what each person's contributions were to the discussion, and the more advanced thinking that occurred for each individual after the discussion. When teaching in a distance learning environment, we adapted this same technique by using digital collaborative slides that each student developed during their breakout room discussions.

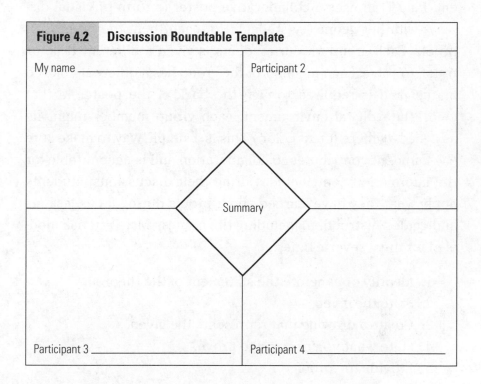

Figure 4.2   Discussion Roundtable Template

We have seen this customized in other content areas. In mathematics, groups are assigned a complex word problem, and each contributor is responsible for proposing a different element to solving the problem. One student determines what the problem is asking them to solve, another creates a visual representation, another calculates the problem, and the fourth links it to a math model. After the discussion, the students independently write a justification for their solution. This team task is further enhanced by reflective conversation within and among teams, which contributes to metacognitive skill building.

Collaborative Posters

Working with their peers to create visual displays helps make students' connections between ideas and information transparent. Pam Tran uses a collaborative poster (a form of visual display) with her geometry students to teach them the process of proofs. Each group of four students is given a different task, or proof, to solve. Each member of the group has a different-colored marker and is required to sign the back of the poster in that color. (In a digital environment, each group member might be assigned a different text color.) This is a simple way to make sure each student contributes to collaboration and is accountable for the information contributed. During their discussions, students apply what they have learned about proofs during focus lessons and guided instruction, including the process Ms. Tran has modeled for them several times:

1. Identify or generate the statement of the theorem.
2. State the given.
3. Create a drawing that represents the given.
4. State what you're going to prove.
5. Provide the proof.

The modeling of this process of solving proofs is critical, and the guided instruction students receive can be used to correct misconceptions and address knowledge gaps; the collaborative learning task requires students to use what they know.

Collaborative posters can be used for different grades and subject areas. For example, a group of 1st graders might create a Venn diagram to identify the similarities and differences between two characters, a group of 6th graders might use a timeline to aid their understanding of the various kingdoms and dynasties in

Egyptian history, and a group of biology students could demonstrate their understanding of cell division by creating a process chart. Because this productive group work activity may promote a task completion mindset, make sure that the teams have time at the beginning to discuss a shared understanding of success and an opportunity to link individual learning goals to group ones.

Reciprocal Teaching

Reciprocal teaching is an instructional strategy in which groups of four students read a piece of text and then engage in a conversation about the text (Palincsar & Brown, 1984). The conversation is structured around four strategies: summarizing, question generating, clarifying, and predicting. As with most collaborative structures, students need practice and modeling before they can use reciprocal teaching with their peers. The approach is most effective when students understand the four comprehension strategies that comprise the conversation (Oczkus, 2018).

Summarizing is a brief written or oral review of the main points of the text. Text can be summarized across sentences, paragraphs, or the selection as a whole. When students first use reciprocal teaching, they typically focus on sentence- and paragraph-level summaries. As they become skilled with procedures, they begin to summarize at the paragraph and passage levels.

Question generating focuses students on inquiry and investigation. As students generate questions, they identify the type of information that is important enough to provide the basis for a question. During the question portion of a reciprocal teaching discussion, students often answer one another's questions and thus engage in conversations that extend beyond the text. Over time, and with modeling and practice, students learn to generate questions at many levels of complexity. For example, students might learn to ask the four types of questions common in question–answer relationships (i.e., right there, think and search, author and you, on your own; Raphael et al., 2006), or they might focus on text-dependent questions such as key details, vocabulary and text structure, author's purpose, inferences, or opinions and arguments (Fisher et al., 2015).

Clarifying is a metacognitive activity in which students learn to notice things that they don't understand. During the discussion about the text, students ask for clarification on components of the text that blocked their comprehension. Early in the use of reciprocal teaching, students often seek clarification on individual words. Over time, students will also clarify ideas that confuse them, missing background information that others might have, and unfamiliar experiences discussed in the text. In addition, with modeling and practice, students can incorporate another comprehension strategy, visualizing, into their clarifying. One of the ways to teach readers this strategy is to tell them to "make a movie in your mind" as they read.

Predicting is the process of making an educated guess, based on the best information available, about what might happen next. In order to make predictions successfully, students must activate both background and prior knowledge, pay attention to what the author has said, and make inferences. Predicting also keeps readers engaged with the text, as they want to read further to determine if their predictions are correct.

For an example of how reciprocal teaching can help students advance toward independent learning, consider what went on in Tony Nelson's 4th grade science class during a unit focused on nutrition, exercise, and fitness. Following a series of focus lessons and guided instructional events, students were ready to work in collaborative groups. Each productive work group had copies of the "Choose My Plate" informational poster produced by the U.S. Department of Agriculture (www.myplate.gov/). They used summarizing, questioning, clarifying, and predicting to read and discuss this text, and the members of each group developed their own notes regarding each of these elements of reciprocal teaching. This text generated more questions for the groups than anything else in the unit. As an extension, Mr. Nelson asked his students to select one of their group's questions for further research. Angel's group identified a number of them for further inquiry:

- What is a "healthy" food item? An "unhealthy" food item?
- Why is it important that we eat healthfully?
- How many food items did we eat last night that were considered healthy? Unhealthy?
- Do you think you are eating healthy meals according to the diagram?
- What might you want to change to eat better?
- Is it possible to eat better at home? At school?

Angel selected the final question and began her quest for the answer through internet searches and additional print and digital readings, looking for possible answers. Over the weeklong investigation of their questions, students drafted responses, met with Mr. Nelson for editing sessions, met with peers for feedback, and read extensively. Angel's answer was complex and read, in part, like this:

> It is possible to eat better—if you want to, and if adults help. With some education, parents and cafeteria staff could prepare very healthy meals. This would mean that students would have to stop begging for unhealthy meals, like fried food. To eat healthier, students need choices, and they need to make good choices.

In the case of Mr. Nelson's lesson, all the students were reading and commenting on the same piece of text. There are other times, however, when you want students to consolidate their understanding across multiple documents or artifacts. To accomplish this, use a jigsaw arrangement to promote synthesis of knowledge.

Jigsaw

In this collaborative learning routine, each group member learns some unique material and then teaches it to other group members. Elliot Aronson developed the jigsaw classroom in 1971 in Austin, Texas, in response to the kind of in-class conflict he was seeing (see www.jigsaw.org). In most classrooms at the time, students competed against one another for grades and had few opportunities and little motivation to collaborate. Aronson's goal was to restructure the classroom for positive interdependence.

Although Aronson's original work was conducted in a 5th grade classroom, this approach can be used across grade levels and content areas. History teacher Javier Vaca routinely uses the jigsaw method when students are learning about primary and secondary source materials. In their home groups, students gain knowledge about individual documents and then share this knowledge with the other members of their group. But each student is also a member of an expert group, where students jointly build their expertise about a particular document. The expert group is key to making jigsaw work, as individuals benefit from the collective wisdom of the group. This also ensures that a group is not inadvertently left behind due to the fact that an individual assigned to a document did not understand it.

Often overlooked is the most valuable step when it comes to building the student learning community: having individuals return a second time to their expert group to consider how the content they were responsible for fits into the larger topic. This part-to-whole approach encourages students not only to engage in critical thinking about the content but also to enrich the learning experience of everyone in their learning community. Little wonder that with an effect size of 1.20, jigsaw (done properly) has the highest effect size of all instructional strategies (www.visiblelearningmetax.com).

During a unit on the American home front war effort during World War II, Cassandra worked within an expert group of students assigned to analyze the text from Franklin Delano Roosevelt's fireside chat from February 23, 1942, "On the Progress of the War." Cassandra's group chunked the long text and used a reciprocal teaching approach to discuss it in depth. Lex, a member of the expert group, commented on FDR's opening allusion to Washington's troops at Valley Forge; the group consulted a map in order to better understand troop movements and critical territories. Cassandra drew their attention back to the end of the radio broadcast text, noting that the president was beseeching his listeners to focus their efforts on increasing military supply production and set aside labor disputes in order to meet demand.

Forty-five minutes later, Cassandra rejoined her home group, made up of students who had become experts on other documents. During the remainder of this class period and the next day's as well, she and her home group members taught one another about the war bond effort and viewed several film clips used in movie theater campaigns. They read a secondary source describing the rationing program for civilians and viewed images of rationing coupons. One student in their home group, Mario, taught them about the victory garden program promoted as a means for Americans to supplement their rationed canned goods. He noted that he had learned that victory gardens were not confined to the American war effort and that many countries had promoted their use as far back as World War I. "I think it's interesting that they coupled this with rationing and made sure that people knew their sacrifices were to support the war effort," he said. After everyone's presentations, students returned a second time to their expert groups to consider how their document contributed to a larger picture of a country in crisis. The over-all result was that the groups moved to a synthesis of these documents. The conclusions they drew included the fact that these efforts were necessary from an economic standpoint but were strategically presented to the American people as a way to actively contribute to a cause. As Cassandra explained to Mr. Vaca,

> A lot of times people think that individually they don't make much of a difference. It seems like the government placed a lot of effort in getting people involved and keeping them up to date on what was happening. When you're involved, you feel like you can make a sacrifice for the greater good and that it will mean something.

5-Word Summaries

This has been a go-to task for us for years. It's built on the truth that when students first encounter an informational passage or article, they can have a difficult time wading through the details in order to locate the main idea and really get the gist of what the writer wants to communicate. The 5-word summary strategy turns that from an often-frustrating, isolated experience into a col-laborative, discussion-based one that's not only an opportunity to use academic language but also a prime example of leveraging peer support to enhance learning. Here's the process, which can be used in the early elementary grades through high school:

1. After reading the assigned passage, each student makes a list of the five most important words or phrases in the reading.
2. Once students have developed their list, they pair with another student to negotiate a consensus list of five words, merging their individual lists into a new, collabora-tively created one.

3. Each student pair joins another student pair, and these four students repeat the process to generate a new five-word list that all agree upon.

4. These students use their finalized list to compose a summary of the article.

Notice that students perform these negotiations twice—once in a group of two and then again in a group of four. Don't be tempted to pare this back for time. Allowing students to develop confidence with a partner and then advocate for and perhaps modify their perspective within a larger group does more than support a better understanding of what the text means; it also helps to enhance students' sense of what it means to *come to understand.*

We have found this routine to be especially useful as a way to bridge synchronous and asynchronous learning. Students perform the second step in breakout rooms, then the teacher collapses the rooms for the third step. Once the groups have finalized their consensus list of words, they can write their summary asynchronously. The routine is particularly helpful to students who might struggle to complete a summary on their own.

Specialized Routines for Productive Group Work

In addition to the generic productive group work routines we have covered, there are a number of specialized routines that teachers can use to engage students in this kind of collaborative learning. We will consider two such routines, both of which provide students an enhanced opportunity to interact with one another and the content.

Literature Circles and Book Clubs

Literature circles (Daniels, 2001) and book clubs (McMahon et al., 2007) are popular approaches for differentiating reading assignments because they allow for peer-led, small-group discussions of a common text. Students do not read in the presence of others (this is done during independent reading or during asynchronous learning); they gather together to discuss what they have read. The literature circles approach stresses choice and the temporary nature of the groups, as configurations change with the next round of books. Several principles are central to literature circles:

- *Students have choice in the books they read.* These choices are often limited to a list the teacher has compiled (usually chosen because they have a common theme and represent a range of text complexity), but students choose which they will read, sometimes with some "artful teacher guidance" (Daniels, 2006, p. 11). Group formation is then predicated on book choice, which really creates an interest group.
- *Students have a responsibility to themselves and to their peers.* These responsibilities include record keeping, contributing to group discussions, and, of course, keeping up with the assignment. It is hard to hide in a group of six or so when you have not done the reading! Students create their own ground rules and schedule the times they will meet. Once comfortable with the process, groups jointly determine how much they will read before the next meeting.
- *There is increased engagement in these peer-led discussions.* Daniels calls this "airtime," and it stands to reason that in a small group the level of participation is going to increase (2006, p. 11). Drawing a quiet student into the discussion becomes the job of supportive peers, not the teacher.

The social development of these groups can be challenging for students new to the gradual release of responsibility and, thus, accustomed to relying on teacher-directed instruction.

Many teachers initially use role sheets to formalize the social and academic behaviors necessary for effective peer-led discussions. These roles typically align with the content of the discussion, such as Discussion Director, Vocabulary Enricher, and so on. Keep in mind, however, that support for the development of everyone's leadership skills is a condition of student learning communities. Make sure to rotate these roles so that each student develops a broad range of skills. As the year progresses, empower teams to select their own roles. Once students become adept at literature circle discussion, you'll likely see them abandon roles in favor of conversations that have a more natural ebb and flow.

Now, an illustration. Teresa Pelletier's 5th grade students have been participating in literature circles since the beginning of the school year, and they are now in their fourth cycle. Each cycle features a unifying essential question to be answered through whole-class shared reading, as collaborative groups read one of five literature club titles. The essential question for this cycle is "How can an act of courage affect others?" Ms. Pelletier is reading *The Wanderer* by Sharon Creech, a complex text, with the entire class. The students, as part of their literature circles, are also reading one of the following:

- *Esperanza Rising* by Pam Muñoz Ryan
- *Number the Stars* by Lois Lowry
- *The True Confessions of Charlotte Doyle* by Avi
- *The Crossover* by Kwame Alexander
- *Wonder* by R. J. Palacio

Ms. Pelletier selected these books carefully to represent a range of possible answers to the question, including righting an injustice, saving the lives of others, and venturing into new realms. She considered gender, ethnicity, and age, as well as text difficulty (two of the selections are picture books). She previewed each title during a book talk, and students made their top three selections. This allowed her to shape the groups so that they were equally distributed and to match a few students with books that were not significantly above their reading level.

For two weeks, literature circles have met to discuss the readings and then record their reactions in their reading journals. Amira's group is reading *The Crossover;* they end each discussion by revisiting the essential question to see if they have developed an answer. At the end of the two weeks, each student writes an essay about the question, using examples from their literature circle selection and *The Wanderer,* the novel by Sharon Creech that the entire class has read. Amira's essay contains the following paragraph:

> Seeing someone else be courageous can make other people believe they could be courageous, too. Like when Josh and JB [characters in *The Crossover*] had to figure out how to be brothers again when their dad died. That was courage for both of them. When we read *The Wanderer,* there was courage there after the wave almost killed everyone. All the people on the boat start taking care of each other in better ways. Sometimes people think courage is about being brave in a dangerous situation. The characters in these books were courageous with their feelings toward other people.

Labs and Simulations

Labs and simulations are an ideal structure for collaborative learning because they allow for student interaction and inquiry. Labs are most common in science education, but they can also be used in art and physical education. In science classrooms, students should "participate in a range of lab activities to verify known scientific concepts, pose research questions, conceive their own investigations, and create models of natural phenomena" (Singer et al., 2006). Participating in these types of activities, especially within a gradual release of responsibility instructional framework, helps students understand the content.

Consider the following example, from Justin Miller's science class, of students applying what they have learned about electricity in a science lab. In their lab groups, students were given several fruits and vegetables (lemons, potatoes, grapefruit, tomatoes, and oranges), shiny copper pennies, zinc-plated screws, wires with alligator clips, a light-emitting diode (LED) with a low voltage rating, and a multimeter. Their collaborative task was to consolidate the knowledge gained thus far and to light the LED. Once groups had successfully delivered electricity to the LED, they used the multimeter to measure the amount of electricity produced. Thus, the task was twofold: first, use the supplies to make electricity; second, determine which arrangement produced the most electricity. Each student had to form a hypothesis and then work with the group to test it.

Mr. Miller did not simply walk around the room to manage this lab. He knew that this was the ideal time for him to provide guided instruction and push students' thinking to higher levels. He first met with a group of four students whose formative assessment results had indicated they were struggling to grasp the concepts of circuits and conductors. With them, he shared *Electricity* by Laura Parker, part of the Eyewitness book series, calling particular attention to the visual explanation of circuits and conductors on page 22.

Nearby, one of the groups had inserted a penny in one side of the lemon and a zinc-plated screw into the other. They connected the wires to the penny and screw and then lit the LED. Mr. Miller looked up and asked the members of the group if they could make their signal strength any stronger. He also reminded them that they each had to explain, in their science journals, why this worked. Andrew noted in his journal that "when the screw contacted with the citric acid in the lemon, it started two chemical reactions: oxidation and reduction."

Like labs, simulations are used to ensure that learning is applied (Aldrich, 2005; Falloon, 2020). Simulations, both virtual and in person, are becoming more common in social studies, language arts, and other content areas for learning such things as cause and effect. Once the exclusive realm of higher education, simulations have grown in popularity with even very young children as the evidence for their value in promoting transfer expands (Smith, 2014).

In her government class, Janice Fink uses simulations of town hall meetings and congressional voting. During one session, she provided students with a scenario very real to their lives: drag racing on the freeway. She distributed copies of a newspaper article about drag racing, a political cartoon on the subject, a section of the vehicle code, and a proposed amendment to the code, which would criminalize observing drag racing. The room was charged, and students began sharing their opinions about this with one another. Ms. Fink interrupted their conversations and reminded them of the process of a town hall meeting.

She assigned her students roles as mayor, council members, community members, parents of a young adult killed while drag racing, business owners, observers of drag races, three well-known drag racers, and police officers. Ms. Fink reminded her students that the conversation could go in any direction they chose, as long as they respected the town hall process and remained in their roles. In their collaborative groups, students shared their thinking about the proposed law and provided feedback and commentary.

During this time, Ms. Fink met with individual students who needed additional support to make their position known. She also met with the mayor and council members in a small, guided-instruction group to remind them of their role in the discussion and how to manage the town hall meeting. Over several days, with focus lessons, guided instruction, and collaborative learning events, the students were prepared for the simulation.

Janae started the conversation:

Mr. Mayor and Members of the Council: I can't believe that you're thinking of making it a crime to watch drag racing. What could I, the observer, do? Where will it stop? Will it be a crime to observe a house robbery? Will it be a crime to watch someone run a stop sign or light? And who will enforce this rule?

Marvin asked to speak next. His role was "business owner":

I like drag racing, so it doesn't matter what rules you make up.

Ms. Fink interrupted the group and reminded students that they had to be true to their role. To Marvin, she said, "Which business owner's perspective are you speaking from? Think about that. Some business owners might sympathize with what you just said, but others would disagree with you. Maybe you should start over and introduce yourself. That would give us the context for your speech."

Over the course of the town hall meeting, many different opinions were expressed, ideas were challenged, and positions were forwarded. Ms. Fink knew that her students were ready for this simulation because of the structure of her classroom and the work she had done to prepare them.

Assessment During Collaborative Learning

Checking for understanding is essential at each phase of the gradual release of responsibility model (Fisher & Frey, 2015), but it can seem to be more of a challenge during collaborative learning, because so much of the activity is taking place outside the teacher's presence. The key to gathering assessment information is to design individual accountability within productive group work tasks. For example, the students in Mr. Nelson's class chose a question for further research and produced a report. Ms. Tran's geometry students developed a collaborative poster using a format that allowed her to determine the level of participation for each member.

Here are five guiding questions we use to design assessment tasks for collaborative learning (Frey & Fisher, 2011):

1. What evidence do I need in order to make future instructional decisions?
2. What evidence would be most useful for informing guided instruction follow-up?
3. Does this assessment task provide meaningful feedback to the student?
4. Can every member of the group do this assessment task in a meaningful way?
5. If not, in what ways can this assessment task be modified to meet the needs of those students?

Sometimes during productive group work, students will temporarily "forget" what they already know because they are so focused on the newer information they are attempting to apply. Novices are not the best at noticing patterns and marshaling resources to resolve problems. That's precisely what you're looking for during productive group work, because the goal is for them to consolidate their understanding. When you notice that students need to remember what they know, you shift back to guided instruction.

Building Confidence and Competence Through Collaborative Learning

A chief purpose of collaborative learning is for students to consolidate their thinking and knowledge as they confront new and novel tasks. This consolidation process is often termed a *transfer of learning,* as it promotes metacognitive thinking. Transfer of learning results in a notable advancement of a student's ability to use concepts and skills in increasingly independent ways. That said, the collaborative tasks students perform must require them to engage in critical thinking associated with transfer, which Falloon (2020) identifies as follows:

1. Revisiting learned processes and concepts;
2. Comparing prior and current conceptions;
3. Being aware of and analyzing difficulties and differences;
4. Identifying the use and purpose of learned concepts and materials;
5. Handling learned materials or processes in different ways; and
6. Applying learned materials and processes in different circumstances (p. 783).

Collaborative learning has the potential to promote the confidence of learners, especially as they practice the kind of reflective thinking about their own goals and those of the group. Time spent allowing teams to consider their goals and the success criteria provides members with the opportunity to gauge their own confidence and consider it within the context of the group effort needed. In other words, it helps children understand that the success of the group is dependent not on a single member but on the individual contributions each member brings to the task.

Conclusion

Collaborative learning provides a critical bridge in student learning because it allows novice learners to refine their thinking about new concepts and skills. The oral language development in such settings is particularly valuable, because it requires the use of social and academic language in order to accomplish the task. Individual accountability is a hallmark of productive group work, as it minimizes the frustration felt by some students who believe they have shouldered an unfair burden. The configuration of the group is important to its success. Although there are times when student choice or interest groups are useful, in most cases, the grouping should be heterogeneous so as not to impoverish some groups that have fewer collective resources among them. This is just as important for high-achieving students, who tend to collaborate less in groups they perceive as needing less of their help.

5

Independent Learning: Practicing and Applying What Has Been Taught

At some point in every lesson, students need to complete tasks on their own. Sometimes, these independent learning tasks are used at the outset of a lesson to activate background knowledge or check for understanding. Other times, independent learning tasks are used to solidify the learning as students practice and apply what they have been taught. It's important to note that these types of tasks should not be reserved for the end of the lesson or unit, or for homework. In distance and blended learning, these opportunities may occur during asynchronous time. Students need opportunities to practice and apply what they have learned in every lesson. In essence, they need to try the learning on and see how it fits. Of course, students are likely to make mistakes and errors as they work out the fit. Teachers can learn a lot from watching students practice and apply—and can use that information to design additional, targeted learning experiences.

As we have noted previously, it is important for students to consolidate their understanding with peers during collaborative learning. In this chapter, we focus on the role of practice and application, both which require students to spend time working and thinking alone. As Ericsson and colleagues (1993) note, serious study alone, what they call *solitary practice,* is one of the strongest predictors of expert performance. And that's what we want for students: expert performance. The culmination of the gradual release of responsibility is students who

- Own their learning,
- Are self-directed learners,
- Are independent and *inter*dependent rather than dependent, and
- Can apply their learning in a variety of situations.

A common misconception about independent learning is that the ultimate goal is for the student to accurately reiterate or replicate what has been taught. But independent learning is far more complex than that. Yes, students need to reiterate and replicate—that's called practice. But they also need to *apply.* And sometimes they need to struggle and work things out for themselves. Duke (2012) illustrates this point while recounting a music teacher's experience:

> A student in her class was trying to figure out a piano fingering as she was standing beside him watching. After several unsuccessful repetitions, he looked to her and said, "If you were a good teacher, you'd tell me how to do this," whereupon my very astute and skillful grad student replied, "Yes, but because I'm an excellent teacher, I'm going to wait a while longer while you figure it out." Of course, she said that with the informed confidence that her student could in fact figure it out, which he did after the next few attempts. Think about what the student learned from that experience, other than the fact that his

teacher's a hard nose. He discovered that he could figure it out. His moments in the muddle led to his arriving at an advantageous solution, and all of the errors he made along the way actually strengthened the memory of the solution and the path he took in reaching it. (p. 40)

This story captures an important element of independent learning: the teacher was sure that the student's previous learning had properly equipped him to succeed.

The Benefits of Practice and Application

When students are working alone, there are two main goals. The first is for them to practice, and the second is for them to apply. When students apply what they know, they generalize and transfer their understanding to a new situation. As we will see throughout this chapter, there are a number of ways to set students up to apply what they know, and this can happen in school or at home. Application tasks are generally valued tasks, whereas practice seems to be marginalized. But both are important. Students need to practice and apply if they are to really learn.

The familiar expression is "practice makes perfect," but in truth, practice makes permanent. Unfortunately, practice seems to be undervalued in academics, and this mindset takes root in students. For contrast, consider sports and many hours of practice young people are willing to endure each week for the chance to play in the game. Consider the practice young people willingly put into playing a musical instrument they love, or drawing, or dancing. They are convinced that the practice improves their performance, and they value the opportunity to perform well. Can we get the same thing to happen in academic pursuits? If we do, better learning is the likely result.

In terms of practice, there are two factors to keep in mind. The first is spaced practice versus mass practice. You likely remember cramming for a test, perhaps the night before. Once the test was over, you promptly forgot all of the information. If you wanted to remember the information longer term, you might have skipped the marathon session and distributed this practice over time (Hattie & Donoghue, 2016). As we will note in the discussion of homework later in this chapter, spiral reviews are a useful way to provide students with spaced practice.

The second thing to remember about practice is that it needs to be deliberate (Ericsson et al., 1993). Distinct from simple, even mindless repetition, *deliberate practice* requires that the learner focus on the practice activities, work toward a goal, push a bit and struggle, and respond to the feedback that is provided. We will discuss feedback later on as well, but getting students to engage in deliberate practice is important if they are going to develop proficiency with the content.

We recognize that we're making this sound very simple; it's not. Assigning the right type of tasks helps move students to deliberate practice. Think about the word *worksheet*. What comes to mind? For us, it's "shut-up sheets." Worksheets keep students quiet and busy. That's not likely to result in deliberate practice. But as the website Cult of Pedagogy reminds us, there is an entire continuum of worksheets, some of which might be useful in facilitating deliberate practice (see Figure 5.1 for Jennifer Gonzalez's visual recap). In addition, a teacher's attention to goal setting, metacognition, and self-regulation all increase the likelihood that students will engage in deliberate practice. Students need to be taught how to think about their own thinking (*metacognition*) and how to act upon their learning (*self-regulation*).

Metacognition

An awareness of one's own thinking coincides with the age one begins formal schooling (4 years old or so), but this awareness must be purposefully nurtured over a learner's academic career. Metacognition is the learner's mindful acknowledgment of their learning processes, the conditions under which they learn best, and a recognition that learning has occurred (Flavell, 1979). This is truly a lifelong phenomenon and, therefore, not something that can be taught in a handful of lessons or mastered in a semester. It requires ongoing investment.

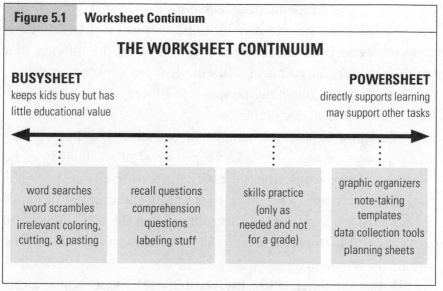

Figure 5.1   Worksheet Continuum

THE WORKSHEET CONTINUUM

BUSYSHEET
keeps kids busy but has little educational value

POWERSHEET
directly supports learning may support other tasks

| word searches word scrambles irrelevant coloring, cutting, & pasting | recall questions comprehension questions labeling stuff | skills practice (only as needed and not for a grade) | graphic organizers note-taking templates data collection tools planning sheets |

Source: From "Frickin' Packets," by J. Gonzalez, March 26, 2018, *Cult of Pedagogy.* Copyright 2018 by Cult of Pedagogy. Used with permission.

The gradual release of responsibility instructional framework supports the development of metacognition in that students are provided with time to recognize that learning has occurred and under what conditions. Work to build this awareness begins during focused instruction, as the teacher thinks aloud (calling attention to the decision-making process), and it extends through guided instruction, as the teacher prompts students to notice what they know and do not know. Students assume more responsibility for their metacognition as they explain their thinking, justify solutions, and listen to the thinking of others in collaborative learning groups.

The goal is for students to independently work to understand their thinking process. Anderson (2002) suggests a series of four questions that challenge learners to move from cognition to metacognition. Teachers can use these questions through a lesson or activity. Metacognitive self-talk can be fostered by encouraging students to use these four questions during both collaborative and independent learning.

"What am I trying to accomplish?" This first question aims to move learners from merely copying a task to identifying that task's intended outcomes. ("This math word problem is asking me to figure out how many people can be served with the number of apple pies at the picnic.")

"What strategies am I using?" After identifying the problem and the goal, the next step is to figure out what strategies can be used to achieve a solution. ("I really need to use two strategies to find the answer. First I have to multiply the number of slices by the total number of pies. That will give me the total number of servings. But then I also have to divide those servings among the people at the picnic.")

"How well am I using the strategies?" Once again, monitoring plays an important role in the acquisition of new learning. This question reminds students that effective use of a skill or strategy comes from pausing from time to time during the process to see how well it's working. ("Before I divide, I need to check to see if what I've multiplied makes sense. Could it be that 8 apple pies could be cut into a total of 64 slices? I also want to check my math. Does $8 \times 8 = 64$?")

"What else could I do to accomplish the goal?" The point of this question is to teach students to think flexibly and avoid getting bogged down in rigid thinking. At this stage of learning, it is common for students to focus on new skills and strategies and temporarily forget previously learned skills and strategies they have at their disposal. By asking "What else could I do?" they remind themselves that those familiar strategies could play a role. ("I'm still not sure I am doing this correctly. One way I can be sure is if I draw a diagram of the pies and the people. We've done diagramming before when we've had tough word problems. I'm going to try that now.")

Whether in mathematics or any other content area, students need to see how to prepare and plan, select an approach, and monitor the execution of their plan. This is especially valuable during independent learning, when students are driving their own progress. Persistence is vital as well, and students who have a metacognitive process can think their way through a difficult patch, get themselves unstuck, and figure it out for themselves.

Self-Regulation

Students need to self-regulate as they engage in independent learning. Self-regulation includes acting upon the metacognitive perceptions they experience during a task, such as rereading a passage when comprehension breaks down, consulting another resource to clarify the meaning of a vaguely understood vocabulary term, or checking their work for errors after completion. These metacognitive behaviors are linked to the learner's intentions and goals, such as finishing the task, doing it well, and receiving positive feedback. In other words, metacognitive awareness is the starting point. The behaviors that follow it constitute a learner's self-regulation.

Time management. Checklists and reminders to use problem-solving questions are a significant way to scaffold students' developing ability to self-regulate. Many teachers build regulatory supports into longer independent learning projects. For example, a 3rd grade teacher may require a daily check-in to gauge progress on a science research report. Young children have difficulty managing time, and these interim checkpoints can be of great help to them.

Task prioritization. Another aspect of self-regulation is prioritizing tasks. Younger students are not especially good at determining which tasks are more difficult and therefore require more attention. Dufresne and Kobasigawa (1989) presented a range of paired words for students in grades 1 through 7 to memorize, and then gave them time to study. The students in the lower grades did not know how to allocate their time to focus on the more difficult items to memorize, which is what the 5th through 7th grade students did. Teachers can support the development of this self-regulatory process by providing directions that identify the more difficult and time-consuming elements of an assignment.

Calibration. A third component of self-regulation during independent learning is calibration, the ability to accurately self-assess in order to affect learning decisions. Calibration is a newer area of research in metacognition and self-regulation, and it focuses primarily on students' knowledge of the gap between where their current performance is and what they hope to achieve (Hattie, 2013). A meta-analysis conducted by Hattie (2009) found that self-reported expectations and self-grading are among the most effective instructional approaches a teacher can use. For example, students in general can accurately predict their score on a test, although this ability declines among students who perform poorly. Why is this? Hattie notes that students who possess inaccurate information are more likely to be overconfident—in other words, they don't know what they don't know. Therefore, they are less able to effectively allocate attention to items in need of further consideration. This inability to calibrate extends to teachers as well. In one series of large-scale studies, elementary teachers underestimated task difficulty by one grade level, whereas high school teachers overestimated task difficulty by one grade level (Hattie et al., 2005).

The vision of a roomful of students silently toiling away on an assignment while the teacher spends the entire time filing papers and putting materials away is wrongheaded. Independent learning, when it occurs in the classroom, should include meta-cognitive supports that encourage growth in self-regulation. The teacher provides this support through feedback on tasks students complete inside and outside the classroom.

Independent Learning During the School Day

There is a wide range of independent learning tasks that students in face-to-face and digital learning environments can engage in when school is in session. Here are a few examples:

- *Journal and essay writing.* Students can respond to prompts that allow them to convey information, entertain readers, argue a perspective, or share an experience.
- *Independent reading.* Students can read from texts that have been assigned or texts that they have selected. They can build background knowledge and vocabulary in doing so and then share their knowledge with others.
- *Designing, drafting, and completing projects.* There are any number of projects students can complete on their own. Although some projects are better suited for collaborative learning, it is appropriate at times for students to complete projects on their own.
- *Performances and presentations.* Sharing with the class or wider audience allows students to practice organization and public speaking skills as well as to receive feedback from peers. Students can record these and post them on the learning management system's discussion board.
- *Preparing for discussions, debates, and Socratic seminars.* In addition to the time spent at home doing some of these activities, students may need time in school to organize themselves and prepare for tasks that require that they interact with others, as would be the case for a debate or class discussion.

- *Research*. Time to find things, including internet searches and visits to the library, is useful for students to investigate a topic as they prepare to use that information for another task, such as writing or debate or presentation.

Independent tasks should allow students to practice and apply their understanding of the content, *not* replicate the work the teacher has done. Take note of the range of things that students might be doing independently. Remind yourself that these are more than tasks; they are opportunities for students to learn from the work they are doing.

Here's an example. The Literacy Design Collaborative (www .LDC.org) has developed useful sets of writing task templates that encourage students to continue to build knowledge during independent learning. The templates are organized by the critical thinking skills the tasks require: *analysis, comparison, evaluation, problem-solution, cause and effect, definition, description, procedural-sequential,* and *synthesis*. For example, one task template for evaluation using research reads as follows:

> After researching _____ (informational texts) on _____ (content), write a/an _____ (essay or substitute) that discusses _____ (content) and evaluates _____ (content). Be sure to support your position with evidence from your research.

Employed in a 5th grade social studies class, the task might be this:

> After researching primary and secondary sources on the American Revolution, write an essay that discusses the American and British perspectives at the time and evaluates the reasons for starting the war. Be sure to support your position with evidence from your research.

When planning independent learning tasks, teachers should consider the following questions (Frey et al., 2010):

1. *What digital and print-based information do students need to* **find**? Identify new content they will need to acquire (e.g., facts, statistics, ideas) and how they'll track down that content (e.g., with a search engine, through a WebQuest, via a personal interview).

2. *What digital and print-based information do students need to* **use**? Identify what students have already created or encountered in class that they will need for task completion (e.g., notes taken, annotations, course readings, video and audio recordings) and the procedures they will follow to use this material appropriately (e.g., to avoid plagiarism, to ensure proper referencing).

3. *What digital and print-based information or products do students need to* **create**? Identify the format or formats they will use to demonstrate their new learning (e.g., digital storytelling, website, presentation, written content).

4. *What digital and print-based information do students need to* **share**? Identify the ways in which students will share their information, learning, or creation with a larger audience (e.g., a review on Amazon.com, YouTube video, blog posting, or presentation).

"Independent" doesn't mean a free-for-all task; the learning in this phase, like all phases, must be purposeful. Asking and answering these four questions is a way that teachers can ensure students have what they need in terms of materials and directions so that they can work on their own to apply learning and don't need to keep asking what to do next. When the task is clear and the materials are readily available, teachers can be more confident that student confusion or stalling suggests they're not yet ready to work on their own and may benefit from cycling back through another phase of the framework. In addition to the planning function they serve, asking these questions supports assessment efforts as well as reteaching.

Independent Learning Beyond the School Day (Homework)

Few topics in education are more contentious than homework. Some love it; others hate it. Research suggests that homework does have a positive effect on achievement, albeit one correlated with the age of the student: the effect is smallest in the elementary school years, grows modestly in middle school, and is most closely linked to achievement in high school (www.visiblelearning metax.com).

Not to be ignored is the impact that homework has on family life. Vatterott (2018) is among those advising teachers to keep developmental, family, and learning concerns in mind. For example, teachers might make younger students' homework assignments *time based* rather than *task based* (e.g., ask kindergartners to complete 10 minutes of nightly homework rather than a particular worksheet). This advice certainly resonates with us. We work in a neighborhood where many students have religious and community obligations on weeknights, and one way we try to help them manage homework is to assign it on a flexible schedule. Homework assignments are given with an expectation that they should be completed sometime during the week, but the specific night is left to the discretion of the student. Not only does this approach help students manage the expectations of home and school, but we believe it more closely parallels the demands of college and career, where task completion planning is an essential skill.

Our primary concern with homework is that it is traditionally assigned too early in the instructional cycle—before students are really ready to assume cognitive responsibility. If you follow the logic of presenting information to students and fostering those skills using a gradient of scaffolds and supports, you'll come to the same conclusion we have: *traditional homework occurs too early in the instructional cycle.* (We said it twice to emphasize the point.) It makes no sense to introduce a topic at 8:20 a.m. and then expect students to be able to apply understanding of that topic alone, away from any support, 10 or 12 hours later. Students who are just learning a new skill—say, learning to convert fractions to decimals—are not going to be able to perform that skill very well on their own. If you release responsibility for this learning too early by making it the basis for a homework assignment, it's likely your students will reveal themselves to be one of four types:

- The *completers,* who do the homework flawlessly because a parent or older sibling was there to provide the necessary scaffolding
- The *neglecters,* who don't do the homework for whatever reason (and you have no idea what that reason is)
- The *pleasers,* who want to make you happy so they do the homework alone, even though they don't really know how and might make a lot of errors
- The *cheaters,* who copy their homework from another student

Doug freely admits to having been in the "cheater" category as a student and argues that behind every cheater is a pleaser who cares about how the teacher feels. He and a friend routinely traded homework on the long bus ride home, with Doug doing the English assignments and his friend taking charge of the mathematics ones.

Think about the consequences here. Think about the faulty data you're getting and how this affects your ability to assess students' learning and take appropriate actions based on the data.

You can't tell how much scaffolding the completers needed. You don't know whether any of the neglecters mastered the skills or not, because you have nothing to look at. While you can analyze the errors of the pleasers, you can't be certain the errors are really their own. What if they are actually cheaters and got help from someone who didn't really understand the material? And finally, you don't know who the cheaters are. So every morning, you review last night's homework, reteaching because some students didn't get it and others didn't do it. And every morning, you fall a bit further behind because you're now regularly repurposing instructional minutes for homework checking and reteaching.

To be clear, we're not homework haters. In fact, we fall into the camp that thinks homework offers valuable opportunities for learning and self-regulation. But we have found that homework works *best* when it's used to support specific aims within the instructional cycle (Fisher & Frey, 2008). For example:

- *Fluency-building* homework allows students to practice skills they know well. Reading for 15 or 20 minutes per night is a great example of fluency building. Timed mathematics facts is another. This is essentially asking students to chart how many multiplication facts they can complete in one minute so they can see their fluency increase over time.
- *Spiral review* homework is designed to activate background knowledge necessary for the new skills or concepts being taught during the school day. For example, during a chemistry unit on thermal conductivity, the homework might focus on previously taught information on covalent and ionic bonds and polarity.
- *Application* homework provides learners with the chance to apply newly learned skills to a new situation. The English teachers at our school assign all students a quarterly homework assignment that requires them to attend a play,

movie, or museum exhibition and write about its connection to their English content learning.

- *Extension* homework requires students to consolidate what they have learned across two or more content areas in order to deepen their knowledge. A favorite example of extension homework is the assignment given to middle school students who had learned about persuasive writing in English class and natural resources in science class to write to their city council with comments on a proposed water desalination plant.

Note that only application homework and extension homework are truly "independent learning" as defined in the gradual release of responsibility instructional framework. Fluency building and spiral review can be completed with peers, as in collaborative learning, or with adult scaffolding, as in guided instruction. Figure 5.2 (see p. 118) offers some reflective questions that can help teachers develop effective homework assignments.

The Teacher's Role in Independent Learning

As students engage in independent learning, the teacher's role is to notice ongoing performance and provide feedback. Feedback is what allows students to calibrate the gap between their current state and where they want to be. It's what helps them make decisions about the allocation of attention and resources and helps them resolve problems when they are stuck. All too often, unfortunately, the feedback students receive does no such thing—primarily because it focuses on current performance to the exclusion of what could or should happen next. Keep in mind that independent learning is not synonymous with perfection; it's the journey to get to perfection. Similarly, grades are not feedback; they may be evaluative, but they do not promote

Figure 5.2	Developing Effective Homework Assignments	
Purpose of Homework	**Characteristics**	**Reflective Questions**
Fluency building	• Multiple opportunities for practice • Focuses on one or two skills • Serves as an access point for other skills or knowledge	1. Do students fully understand how the skill is performed? 2. Is the difficulty level low enough so that they can focus on speed/rate/fluency, instead of how it is performed?
Application	• Allows a skill to be used to solve a problem, or apply a rule or principle • Uses previously learned skill for a new situation	1. What rule or principle will the students use to solve the problem? 2. Do the students possess the background knowledge and prior experiences necessary to understand the new or novel situation?
Spiral review	• Student utilizes previously learned skills or knowledge • Allows student to confirm their understanding and assess their own learning • Related conceptually to current learning	1. What previously taught skills or knowledge are important for future learning and assessment? 2. In what ways will this strengthen students' metacognitive awareness of how well they use skills and knowledge? 3. What previously taught skills or knowledge serve as a basis for current classroom instruction?
Extension	• Potential for development of new understandings • Results in a new product or innovation • Requires the use of a variety of skills or knowledge	1. Does the assignment lead to a new knowledge base or set of concepts? 2. Will the students create a new product or innovation that they have not done before? 3. What skills or knowledge will students require to complete the assignment?

Source: From "Homework and the Gradual Release of Responsibility: Making 'Responsibility' Possible," by D. Fisher & N. Frey, 2008, *English Journal 98*(2), p. 43. Copyright 2008 by the National Council of Teachers of English. Used with permission.

further learning. Feedback occurs during independent learning, not at the end of it.

When we think about how often feedback fails to promote learning, it's instructive to consider Lee's (2009) study comparing 26 middle and high school writing instructors' expressed beliefs about feedback to the actual feedback they provided on student writing. Lee found that these teachers did the following:

- Favored focusing feedback on student strengths but actually focused their feedback primarily on weaknesses and errors
- Expressed a belief that there is more to good writing than accuracy but focused their feedback on language form
- Used error codes even though they confessed their students were not consistently able to decipher, understand, or apply these codes
- Assigned and graded writing as a single attempt, even though they believed that multiple revisions are necessary to develop writing ability
- Continued to provide feedback as they had always done, even though they believed it had little effect

This last point is especially troubling, because it illustrates a certain resignation: teachers have given up on using feedback as a tool for improvement; for many, giving feedback is something they do more out of habit and tradition than for any defined reason. "Students cannot learn from the mistakes," said one teacher in Lee's study (2009, p. 18), yet 91 percent of the written feedback these teachers generated focused on errors.

Types of Feedback to Students

The fact is, like pretty much anything else, feedback to students can either be done very badly or be used quite effectively. In their seminal review of the research on feedback, Hattie and

Timperley (2007) describe four levels of feedback, some more effective than others.

Feedback about the task, sometimes called *corrective feedback,* can be effective, but only when the student's error is due to an incorrect interpretation. When the student lacks knowledge, feedback about the task is ineffective.

Feedback about the processes used in the task is more effective, as it prompts students to analyze the strategies they are using. It also mirrors the metacognitive thinking in teacher think-alouds presented during modeling. For example, saying, "This would be a good time to check the date of this historical document so you can get a better sense of what was occurring politically at the time" provides the learner with a direction to follow.

Feedback about self-regulation generally draws on learners' self-efficacy—their belief in their own ability to act upon their learning. This type of feedback is also very effective, as it can build self-determination, persistence, and resilience in students. "I can see by this lab report you wrote that your hard work and studying are really paying off" is feedback that communicates the learner's control over the learning. Feedback on self-regulation need not be confined to successes, however. Consider how "You're still having trouble with explaining the differences between mitosis and meiosis, so be sure to target this area for study before the exam" directs the student to the error while building a sense of agency.

Feedback about the self as a person, or general praise ("Nice job!"), does not improve learning, build agency, or change behavior. Hattie and Timperley (2007) include this kind of feedback in their article to highlight its ineffectiveness. Even when it is well meaning, feedback about the self as a person can have a negative effect. For example, "You're so smart!" reinforces a fixed mindset of ability that incorrectly leads students to believe that intelligence is innate (Dweck, 2010).

The sum takeaway is that feedback on the process a student used to complete a task promotes metacognition, and feedback focused on the student's actions fosters self-regulation and a sense of autonomy. Corrective feedback about the task is effective if it is presented within the context of the next steps the student can take, and then only when it addresses a misinterpretation of a concept or skill rather than a lack of knowledge. Feedback focused on the student as a person is not effective for promoting learning.

Criteria for Feedback

Knowing the types of feedback that are most useful is an important part of the equation, but even the most effective type of feedback will be useless unless it is timely, specific, understandable, and actionable (Wiggins, 1998).

Timely. Feedback should always be paired as closely as possible to the task itself. We all have memories of receiving feedback from a teacher weeks after submitting an assignment. Any comments that might have supported the metacognitive or self-regulatory elements of learning were negated simply because too much time had passed. Feedback has to reach students when they're still in that learning space.

Specific. Vague or ambiguous feedback leaves the learner bewildered and unsure of what to do next. Give specific feedback about what is correct or what has been done well and about where improvement should occur. As an example, take a look at 3rd grade teacher Elena Anders's feedback on Corrine's diagram of the solar system:

> I can see you've got all the planets in the correct order, and all eight are here. An error I see is that the sizes are not correct. You have Venus and Mercury as the same size, but Mercury is actually much smaller. I'd like for you to reread page 83 in your science book, about the sizes of the planets, and then we'll look at your diagram again.

Ms. Anders's specific feedback alerts Corrine to the elements that are correct as well as those that Corrine *needs* to correct.

Understandable. Whether the feedback is understandable or not can affect its impact on learning. The meaning of feedback can be particularly elusive when the student is young, is learning a new language, or does not share a similar definition of quality as the teacher. Rubrics can be incredibly helpful in these cases, but only when they are shared and discussed in advance of the independent task and not so task-specific that they become prescriptive.

A well-designed rubric defines quality across several dimensions (the columns) and describes a range of execution (the rows). It does not equate a lack of quality exclusively with the absence of an element. For example, it is common in some rubrics for the highest level of excellence to be described using a string of relative adverbs linked to frequency (always/sometimes/never). Although frequency can be a relevant element of quality, it is not the only one. For a student struggling to understand what quality execution looks like, descriptions of "poor" quality that refer to the absence of something are unlikely to be very helpful.

Actionable. Finally, feedback should result in action—and by now, we hope you agree that this criterion is the most important. Feedback should be such that the student knows what to do next and has the opportunity to do it. Part of the vision statement of our high school in San Diego is that it is never too late to learn (Fisher et al., 2012). Although we realize that time is finite and that the school year does eventually end, policy and practice dictate that assignments and competencies (assessments) be constructed to allow for revision and retakes.

At our school, building in time for post-feedback action requires teachers to think about timelines and the scheduling of units of instruction. It also requires that there be structures in place to make this additional planning work possible. We have committed to sustaining instruction until all students have met the criteria for mastery, which means teachers must think very carefully about differentiation. What should occur for students who are learning more quickly and would benefit from further extension? How do we ensure there is time and space for students who need more attention? In classrooms at our school, differentiation commonly happens during collaborative learning. While some students are receiving more teacher-directed instruction, others are extending and deepening their knowledge as they pursue even higher learning targets. Just because students have met the 6th grade social studies standards regarding ancient Mesopotamia doesn't mean the topic's exhausted. How about challenging those students to link what they have learned in class to the geopolitical climate of today?

It's not just students who benefit from good feedback. The practice of making feedback timely, specific, understandable, and actionable benefits teachers' instructional practices enormously. Think of the feedback you give as data for you to utilize. The challenge is to make feedback work for you as an instructor in a way that's similar to how it works for your learners.

Assessment During Independent Learning

Each of the phases of instruction we have looked at so far incorporates some means of checking for understanding. To recap:

- During *focused instruction,* teachers indicate where students are going in their learning by establishing the purpose, modeling and thinking aloud as an expert, and noticing students' initial understandings.
- During *guided instruction,* teachers utilize what they have noticed to scaffold student understanding through questions, prompts, and cues.

- During *collaborative learning,* teachers gauge how well students appear to be consolidating and extending their learning and provide course corrections as needed.
- During *independent learning,* the teacher's role is to check in with students as they move forward on their own, noticing this progress and ensuring students receive feedback that serves to refine and deepen understanding.

Thus far, we have focused on the use of assessments to make instructional decisions. Of course, teachers can also assess learning to determine where students are in their learning journey and then report that information to students and their families on report cards and transcripts. By and large, these assessments are conducted individually.

Building Confidence and Competence Through Independent Learning

As we noted in the outset of this chapter, independent learning is time that is ripe for students' identity and agency development as well for growing self-regulation. We have spent considerable time on self-regulation and metacognition, so we'll focus here on identity and agency.

During independent learning, as students practice and apply, they tell themselves stories about themselves as learners. When the tasks are complex, students can persevere or quit, which makes us think about growth and fixed mindsets (Dweck, 2007). Importantly, this is not a dichotomy, meaning that a student either has a fixed or a growth mindset. Rather, there are triggers that move students along the continuum between fixed and growth. Importantly, there are times when a fixed mindset is the right mindset to have. When students learn to recognize their triggers, they are much more likely to develop strategies that are useful for learning.

Conclusion

As we have noted, independent learning is *not* "do-it-yourself school." Students should be engaged in tasks that require them to practice and apply what they have learned. Ideally, these tasks encourage students to ask new questions about the world around them. Independent learning should build students' metacognitive skills while allowing the teacher to determine areas of additional instructional need.

As Cain (2012) notes, "If solitude is an important key to creativity—then we might all want to develop a taste for it. We'd want to teach our kids to work independently" (p. 75). Given the demands on students, they must learn to rally their experience, prioritize their tasks, and get to work. When they do so, we will have successfully released responsibility (at least for some amount of content) to our students, equipping them to develop the expertise they will need to succeed in college, their career, and life.

6

Implementing the Gradual Release of Responsibility Instructional Framework

Perhaps the gradual release of responsibility instructional framework we have described is similar to the instructional design process you already use in your classroom; perhaps it is quite different. In this final chapter, we will focus on issues of implementation, particularly planning with and introducing this framework to your students. We will also address what peers and administrators should look for in a classroom structured in this way. And, finally, we will share some important questions to ask yourself as you implement a gradual release of responsibility model in your own classroom.

Although we have presented this framework in a sequential manner, remember that implementation is not a linear process. It is not necessary to march directly from focused instruction to guided instruction and then to collaborative learning, with independent learning held until the very end of the lesson or unit. A given lesson may start with any phase of the instructional framework, as when a lesson begins with an inquiry-based col-laborative learning task. Likewise, certain instructional moves may occur multiple times within the same lesson, as when a teacher establishes several different purposes to reflect a shift in instructional focus from one concept or skill to another. Remember, learning is recursive and iterative, and every lesson occurs within a larger instructional context. Students will continually need to recall, apply, and extend existing skills and knowledge as part of the process of acquiring new skills and knowledge.

Gradual Release of Responsibility Is Consistent with Other Research-Based Approaches

The gradual release of responsibility instructional framework is based on, and complementary with, several other instructional considerations—differentiation among them. And while this book has focused primarily on *instruction,* we recognize that instruction is only one leg of the three-legged stool that supports the learning process. Curriculum planning and content and assessment are also essential considerations in the teaching and learning process.

Although we have noted within the previous chapters the opportunities to differentiate instruction, employ backward design, build social-emotional competency, and assess student learning within the model's specific phases, we want to take some time here for a bigger-picture look at how these approaches operate in conjunction with the gradual release of responsibility.

Differentiated Instruction and Gradual Release of Responsibility

Carol Tomlinson's (2014) framework for differentiation describes a process for considering the learning preferences, abilities, and interests of learners in order to create educational experiences that balance challenge with success. As we discussed in Chapter 3, these experiences can be differentiated in one or more aspects of the curriculum: content, process, and product. As Tomlinson and others (e.g., Benjamin, 2002) have noted, some educators see the implementation of differentiated instruction as problematic because their reliance on whole-group instruction doesn't allow time for students to work at different rates, on a variety of topics, or with a range of materials.

The gradual release of responsibility model has been our solution to the logistics of differentiation. Focused instruction provides time to introduce new concepts for all students and to ensure they are all exposed to grade-level thinking. It is in the guided instruction, collaborative learning, and independent learning phases of the framework that differentiation takes place. We can group students homogeneously for guided instruction that is customized to their learning needs, then regroup them heterogeneously for peer learning. At times, collaborative learning also becomes homogeneous, as when students are grouped by interest or task preference. Learners also work independently to demonstrate their mastery of a concept or skill. Learning contracts, curriculum compacting, and tiered assignments and tests all factor into the educational experiences of our students.

Understanding by Design and Gradual Release of Responsibility

The Understanding by Design (UbD) unit- and lesson-planning process developed by Grant Wiggins and Jay McTighe (2005) features three major components:

- Identifying desired results
- Determining acceptable evidence
- Planning learning experiences and instruction

Determining the enduring understandings of learning is invaluable in developing units of study. In particular, the essential questions posed throughout a unit keep us and our students centered on the purpose of the learning. The process's tools also help us to plan the assessments we will use.

The gradual release of responsibility instructional framework aligns well with the third step in the UbD process: planning learning experiences and instruction. The recursive aspects of the framework provide teachers with an instructional design process that allows them to plan learning experiences that gradually transfer the cognitive load to students and differentiate those lessons more effectively over time.

Social and Emotional Learning and Gradual Release of Responsibility

Every lesson we teach provides an opportunity to develop students' social and emotional skills. And every lesson we teach also has the potential to thwart students' social and emotional development. As you reflect back on the various classroom examples we have shared, did you notice that teachers were building students' agency and identity? In each lesson, students' sense of self and the ways in which their efforts resulted in learning was reinforced. Of course, well-meaning teachers can fail to attribute success to students' efforts and inadvertently prevent them from developing a strong sense of agency.

As noted in Chapter 4, deliberately planned collaborative learning experiences are excellent ways to build students' social skills, communication skills, and peer relationship skills. If we want these skills to develop, we must provide students opportunities to practice them, make mistakes, receive feedback, and try again. If you give up on collaborative learning, it's unlikely that your students will have sufficient practice with the peers to develop the interpersonal social skills necessary to work effectively with others and experience the deep and lasting benefits of learning in community.

Self-regulation is an important mindset that develops across many lessons. As we release responsibility to students and ensure that they assume increased responsibility, we can help them develop the regulatory skills needed to be successful. These regulatory skills are both cognitive and emotional. For example, when you make an error, how do you respond? When students find a mistake you've made, how do you react? Your behaviors serve as a model for students about how to respond to potentially frustrating and embarrassing situations. The same is true when you are excited or experience any other of the range of emotions humans experience. Students are looking to you to see how you respond so that they can try on these behaviors. Further, as you share texts with students, you can comment about the ways in which people in those texts respond to various situations. Try naming the emotions that characters or subjects experience and note how they respond to those emotions. Make this a regular part of the modeling you do for students every day.

As we have noted in another publication of ours, all learning is social and emotional (Smith et al., 2019). No lesson is neutral; each has the power to promote both academic development and social and emotional development. The gradual release of responsibility supports students' developing set of skills across those domains.

Assessment and Gradual Release of Responsibility

We use assessment for many reasons:

- To assist student learning
- To identify students' strengths and weaknesses
- To assess the effectiveness of a particular instructional strategy
- To assess and improve the effectiveness of curriculum programs

- To assess and improve teaching effectiveness
- To provide data that assist in decision making
- To communicate with and involve parents (Kellough & Kellough, 1999, pp. 418–419)

Yes, there are many reasons to use assessment data, but we take exception to the idea that a given assessment is either formative or summative. This is a false dichotomy. In fact, we would argue there is no such thing as "a formative assessment." Teachers use assessment data to make decisions, and the same tool can be used for a variety of purposes. Nothing within the nature of the tool makes it formative or summative; what matters is the way a skilled teacher uses the information the tool generates. Maybe you've heard the analogy that when a chef tastes the soup, it's formative (*What else does this soup need?*), and when the restaurant patron tastes the soup, it's summative (*Is the soup good or bad?*). But sitting at a restaurant and tasting your soup, have you never added salt? Or pepper? Or Tabasco? Every assessment can be formative if the data it generates lead to informed action.

When teachers are gradually releasing responsibility to students, assessment is critical. For example, effective guided instruction is dependent on insight into students' learning status; it's how teachers form groups and how they decide what to teach to these groups. Teachers can use assessment data to flexibly group students using a *situational* process, meaning that students are taught first and then grouped for reteaching or extension, based on the most current information. Focused instruction should also be based on the evidence of student learning that has been collected and analyzed. In fact, there is no aspect of the gradual release of responsibility that neglects assessment information. The products students create during collaborative learning are excellent fodder for assessment. Listening to students during guided instruction or examining their independent work provides teachers with information that they can use to make future instructional decisions. Assessment is the engine that drives the whole process.

Planning with the Gradual Release of Responsibility Instructional Framework

After identifying units of study, teachers plan a series of lessons. A number of different tools can support the thoughtful engagement required by our framework's structured teaching. Our lesson plan template (see Figure 6.1), for example, contains guiding questions to assist in planning. Figure 6.2 shows a lesson plan that Brandon Carmichael developed for his middle school social studies students, using our template. Let's take a look at both the template and what Mr. Carmichael has done with it.

Topic/theme and standards. The unit of study is on immigration and the immigrant experience, which is part of the California 8th grade standards' focus on the American economy and the Industrial Revolution. This unit also integrates several 8th grade Common Core State Standards in ELA/literacy—specifically, standards RI.8.1, RI.8.4, RI.8.5, SL.8.1, and SL.8.2.

Essential question. An essential question reminds students of the overarching purpose of learning concepts. In this case, students are asked to consider the ways in which immigrants have contributed to America's economy and how immigrants' experiences are similar.

Purposes. Mr. Carmichael has identified the learning that his students need as they progress toward meeting the standard.

Focused instruction. Mr. Carmichael planned three different episodes of focused instruction. He will read aloud to his students, modeling his thinking about a text. He will model his thinking about finding additional information, and then model the use of a document analysis tool produced by the National Archives.

Figure 6.1   Lesson Plan Template

Topic/Theme/Unit:	Purpose(s)—Content, Language, and Social:	Materials/Resources:
Standards Addressed:		
Essential Questions:		

FOCUSED INSTRUCTION	"I DO IT"
How will you...	
❑ Make lesson purposes (content–language–social) clear to your students?	
❑ Connect to prior learning?	
❑ Ensure relevance and interest in the content?	
❑ Model and demonstrate?	
❑ Notice what students are learning and still need to learn?	
❑ Provide multiple explanations for new concepts?	
❑ Allow for student interaction?	

(continued)

Figure 6.1   Lesson Plan Template—*(continued)*

"WE DO IT"

GUIDED INSTRUCTION

How will you...

❏ Know that each student thought through and formulated a response to questions?

❏ Prompt and cue as needed?

❏ Allow students a variety of methods and modalities in which to respond?

❏ Assist students in processing information?

"YOU DO IT TOGETHER"

COLLABORATIVE LEARNING

How will you...

❏ Provide a task/experience that encourages student dialogue?

❏ Create/sustain relational conditions to empower their learning?

❏ Help students establish a shared agreement of success?

❏ Promote intentional learning?

❏ Encourage students to leverage peer supports?

❏ Foster leadership skills?

"YOU DO IT ALONE"

INDEPENDENT LEARNING

How will you . . .

☐ Intervene with students who are not ready to move on?

☐ Assess to determine who has mastered content and who needs further assistance?

☐ Extend the lesson for those who are ready to move on?

☐ Support students in connecting concepts to future lessons and in exploring real-life applications?

☐ Provide opportunities for students to self-assess?

☐ Offer opportunities for students to extend their learning?

☐ Endorse students' independent learning or more in-depth study of content?

ASSESSMENTS

Focused Instruction:

Guided Instruction:

Collaborative Learning:

Independent Learning:

Figure 6.2 Sample Lesson Plan

Topic/Theme/Unit:
Immigration and the Immigrant Experience

Purpose(s)—Content, Language, and Social:
Content Goal: Understand that immigration in America is long-standing and complicated.
Language Goals: Interpret two types of documents: (1) a written report (secondary source) and (2) images (photographs); practice writing a conversation; complete "I Am" poem.
Social Goals: Equitable participation and openness to other points of view.

Materials/Resources:
Textbook
Copies/digital access to the following:
- "The Peopling of America, 1830–1930" timeline and commentary downloaded from www .ellisisland.org
- The written document analysis and photo analysis worksheets from www.archives.gov
- Photographs of Ellis Island and Angel Island immigrants
- "Brief on Appeal" and "Angel Island Poem #32"
- "Mexican Workers Await Legal Employment in the United States, Mexicali (Mexico)" and "Library of Congress (LOC) Mexican Immigration"
- "Children at work" images from http:// www.archives.gov/education/lessons/ hine-photos/#documents

Standards Addressed:
California History–Social Science Content Standards
Chronological & Spatial Thinking 1: Students explain how major events are related to one another over time.
8.12: Students analyze the transformation of the American Economy and the changing social and political conditions in the United States in response to the Industrial Revolution.

Common Core ELA/Literacy Standards
Reading Informational Text: Key Ideas and Details
RI.8.1: Cite the textual evidence that most strongly supports an analysis of what the text says explicitly as well as inferences drawn from the text.
Reading Informational Text: Craft and Structure
RI.8.4: Determine the meaning of words and phrases as they are used in a text, including figurative, connotative, and technical meanings; analyze the impact of specific word choices on meaning and tone, including analogies or allusions to other texts.
RI.8.5: Analyze in detail the structure of a specific paragraph in a text, including the role of particular sentences in developing and refining a key concept.
Speaking and Listening: Comprehension and Collaboration

SL.8.1: Engage effectively in a range of collaborative discussions (one-on-one, in groups, and teacher-led) with diverse partners on grade 8 topics, texts, and issues, building on others' ideas and expressing their own clearly.
SL.8.2: Analyze the purpose of information presented in diverse media and formats (e.g., visually, quantitatively, orally) and evaluate the motives (e.g., social, commercial, political) behind its presentation.

Essential Questions:

How have immigrants contributed to America's economy?

How are immigrants' experiences similar?

FOCUSED INSTRUCTION

How will you . . .

☑ Make lesson purposes (content–language–social) clear to your students?

☑ Connect to prior learning?

☑ Ensure relevance and interest in the content?

☑ Model and demonstrate?

☑ Notice what students are learning and still need to learn?

☑ Provide multiple explanations for new concepts?

☑ Allow for student interaction?

"I DO IT"

Teacher shares the purpose with students and checks their understanding by asking for random students to retell the purpose. Teacher notes the relevance of this learning, given the continued debates about immigration. Teacher also notes the learning thus far related to immigration policies and history.

Teacher reads aloud an overview of U.S. immigration and immigration patterns from the Ellis Island web page ("The Peopling of America, 1830–1930"). All students receive a copy to follow along with. Read the selection twice, once straight through to get the overall ideas and a second time with an emphasis on making understanding and questions transparent.

For the second read-aloud, teacher models metacognition strategies, thinking aloud about (1) what documents would help build a better understanding of the immigrant experience, and (2) if the experience was the same for immigrants entering the United States through Ellis Island, through the West Coast, and from the southern borders of California, Arizona, and Texas.

Teacher displays the resources each of the groups will be receiving to provide a bigger picture of the work for the day, and then assigns the groups their particular document.

Teacher makes connection between the new tool (a photo analysis worksheet from the National Archives (with a previously used analysis tool, the written document analysis worksheet from same). Students talk with one another about the photo analysis.

(continued)

Figure 6.2 Sample Lesson Plan—*(continued)*

GUIDED INSTRUCTION	"WE DO IT"
How will you . . . ☑ Know that each student thought through and formulated a response to questions? ☑ Prompt and cue as needed? ☑ Allow students a variety of methods and modalities in which to respond? ☑ Assist students in processing information?	**Whole-Group Guided Instruction** Teacher reviews purpose and use of the photo analysis worksheet. Teacher discusses and defines two main aspects of interpretation: (1) observation and (2) speculation/interpretation. **Small-Group Guided Instruction** The group evaluates two pictures, one of immigrants arriving at Ellis Island and another of immigrants landing at Angel Island. 1. Students complete a photo analysis worksheet for each picture. 2. Students discuss similarities and differences between the two pictures. 3. Students write a paragraph on the back of the photo analysis worksheet reflecting on this prompt: "Based on these two pictures, the people are prepared to work." Each member will be responsible for reporting on the group's work. **Small-Group Guided Instruction** The group evaluates two documents: "Brief on Appeal" and "Angel Island Poem #32." 1. Students complete a document analysis worksheet for each document. 2. Students highlight and discuss any words they find in the documents they believe are "loaded" or point to evidence of the author having a slanted or predisposed social, commercial, or political view of the situation described. 3. Students chart (on an overhead transparency) five specific words they discussed and prepare to present these ideas to the class, via a spokesperson. **Small-Group Guided Instruction** "As needed" error analysis based on difficulty reading textbook-like secondary sources. 1. Students examine the documents "Mexican Workers Await Legal Employment in the United States, Mexicali (Mexico)" and "Library of Congress (LOC) Mexican Immigration." 2. Students highlight words they don't understand and main ideas. 3. Students number the ideas in order; how does the author use one sentence or idea as a basis for the next point? 4. With a partner, students complete a silent (written) conversation.

Small-Group Guided Instruction

"As needed" misconception analysis based on previous use of the document analysis worksheet.

1. Students review "Children at Work" (from the textbook), an illustration from the textbook, and a "children at work" image from the National Archives.
2. Teacher assists students in completing the document textbook example (text and images).
3. Students complete a photograph analysis worksheet analyzing the image from the National Archives.
4. Students complete an "I Am" poem.

COLLABORATIVE LEARNING

How will you....
☑ Provide a task/experience that encourages student dialogue?
☑ Create/sustain relational conditions to empower their learning?
☑ Help students establish a shared agreement of success?
☑ Promote intentional learning?
☑ Encourage students to leverage peer supports?
☑ Foster leadership skills?

"YOU DO IT TOGETHER"

Before engaging in the tasks, groups determine internal roles and responsibilities. Students are provided with accountable talk frames to ask questions of one another, probe thinking, and engage in argumentation.

Collaborative Task 1: One member from each small group explains one point from one of the documents or photographs examined. Together, the collaborative group completes the sentence: "Immigrants enter America with the expectation…"

Collaborative Task 2: One member from each small group explains one point from one of the documents or photographs examined. Students create a thesis statement that presents the immigrants' point of view and justifies immigrating; what were the "pull factors" for immigrants?

Collaborative Task 3: One member from each small group explains one point from one of the documents or photographs examined. Students agree on one major point to complete the sentence: "One reason people come to America is…"

Collaborative Task 4: One member from each small group explains one point from one of the documents or photographs examined. Students create a thesis statement that reflects a valid point of view from an immigrant official denying entry on the West Coast.

(continued)

Figure 6.2   Sample Lesson Plan—*(continued)*

INDEPENDENT LEARNING

How will you...

☑ Intervene with students who are not ready to move on?

☑ Assess to determine who has mastered content and who needs further assistance?

☑ Extend the lesson for those who are ready to move on?

☑ Support students in connecting concepts to future lessons and in exploring real-life applications?

☑ Provide opportunities for students to self-assess?

☑ Offer opportunities for students to extend their learning?

☑ Endorse students' independent learning or more in-depth study of content?

"YOU DO IT ALONE"

Independent Task 1: Students complete "silent conversation" ticket out the door: "I Am" poem.

Independent Task 2: Students read the textbook selection on immigration in the United States and prepare Cornell notes.

Independent Task 3: Students ready to move on watch a History Channel video and then prepare and deliver a peer lesson based on the video content.

Students who are not ready to move on will receive additional guided instruction.

ASSESSMENTS

Exit tickets (2)

Short essay explaining the benefits and challenges of immigration

Essay identifying the benefits of immigration in the late 19th century

Quiz on immigration and the Industrial Revolution

Source: Developed by the Santa Clara County Office of Education, Santa Clara, California. Adapted with permission.

Guided instruction. Mr. Carmichael has planned several guided instruction lessons because he doesn't do the majority of his teaching to the whole group. He has found that time spent with smaller groups of students yields great rewards because he can be much more precise. His first guided lesson is a whole-group one, because he wants to be sure all students understand the tool they will be using in their own analysis. In the smaller groups, he guides students' thinking, scaffolding it through prompts and cues about the documents they are investigating.

Collaborative learning. Collaborative learning will be going on at the same time as guided instruction, so Mr. Carmichael has designed a series of activities that will extend over a few days. He knows that initial collaborative learning must be easy enough for students to complete together, so he has them work in teams on a more familiar task. Over the course of the lesson, students will collaborate on increasingly complex tasks that allow them to consolidate their understanding of the content. Take note of the elements that address student learning communities, especially in fostering relational and leadership skills.

Independent learning. Repetition and reinforcement are key to long-term retention of concepts and skills, so Mr. Carmichael plans to check in on students' application through three independent learning tasks: an exit slip after the first day of instruction on what they learned, an "I Am" poem, and note taking from their textbook. This gives him further insight into who understands the concepts and who still needs instruction.

Assessments. Mr. Carmichael has designed an instructional plan that incorporates exit slips, products from the guided instruction lessons, homework, and a short essay. This provides him with the variety and authenticity he seeks, and the different tasks communicate strongly to his students that learning history is more than memorizing facts and dates. His assessments of mastery include an end-of-chapter test from the teacher's guide accompanying the textbook series and an essay addressing the essential question.

What School Leaders Should Look for in a Gradual Release of Responsibility Classroom

As schools and districts implement the gradual release model in their classrooms, it is important to monitor indicators of success. As with UbD, identifying end results and determining acceptable evidence are essential to achieving desired outcomes (Wiggins & McTighe, 2005). Figure 6.3 provides a rubric administrators and instructional coaches can use to support teachers who are implementing a gradual release of responsibility framework.

Questions a Teacher Should Ask

Determining where to begin in implementing a gradual release of responsibility can be daunting. We have developed these guiding questions as a way to support your efforts to integrate the framework into your existing instructional design.

Have I modeled things I expect students to do collaboratively and independently?

Many teachers assume that effective collaborative and independent learning will take care of itself, but we have discovered that explicit direction in how to work collaboratively and independently is a linchpin in a successful gradual release of responsibility classroom.

For this reason, during the first 20 days of the school year or semester, we devote some time each class period to building our students' capacity to work collaboratively and independently. We provide focused instruction on the tasks they will need to do, such as using the classroom computers, applying a mnemonic for writing in-class essays, participating in collaborative groups,

Figure 6.3   Gradual Release of Responsibility Quality Indicators

Quality Indicator	Phase 1: Focused Instruction			
	Proficient – 4	Skillful – 3	Approaching – 2	Minimal – 1
Lesson contains content, language, and social purposes and is based on formative assessment.	• Lesson is explicitly presented through content, language, and social purposes, which are based on content standards and language demands of the task as well as students' assessed needs.	• Purposes are stated and address students' needs identified via formative assessments but are not well connected to content standards or language demands of the task.	• Only one purpose is stated (i.e., content, language, or social purpose is missing), or purpose is not relevant for students. Some type of assessment has been used to design instruction.	• No content or language purpose is stated or implied. There is no evidence of formative assessment to plan instruction.
Students can explain purposes in their own words: **what** they are learning, **how** they show their learning, and **why** they need to learn this lesson.	• Randomly selected students can explain or demonstrate how the stated purposes relate to their own learning.	• Students can accurately restate the purposes of the lesson but lack a clear understanding of why they are being taught the content.	• Students can restate portions of the purposes of the lesson but lack an understanding of why they are being taught the content.	• Students are unable to correctly state the purposes of the lesson.
Teacher provides an authentic model or demonstration while noticing student responses.	• Modeling includes naming task or strategy, explaining when used, using analogies to link to new learning. • Teacher demonstrates task or strategy, alerts for errors to avoid, shows how applied to check for accuracy. • Modeling consistently contains "I" statements and metacognitive examples. • The teacher notices how students respond and addresses student responses.	• Modeling contains all the indicators (naming, explaining, analogies, demonstration, errors to avoid, and checking), but the teacher only uses some "I" statements. • Metacognition is limited. • The teacher notices how students respond but does not address student responses.	• Modeling contains some indicators (naming, explaining), but the teacher directs students through the use of "you" statements and does not use metacognitive statements to further student understanding. • The teacher does not notice how students respond.	• Modeling contains few indicators. Teacher uses "you" or "we" statements that focus on processes, not thinking. • Student responses are ignored.

(continued)

Figure 6.3   Gradual Release of Responsibility Quality Indicators—*(continued)*

Phase 2: Guided Instruction

Quality Indicator	Proficient – 4	Skillful – 3	Approaching – 2	Minimal – 1
Teacher scaffolds support for students using questions, prompts, and cues.	• Teacher poses questions, asks for clarification; if response is incorrect, directs student to previous learning via prompt. If response still incorrect, provides cues before moving to reinstruction.	• Teacher poses question, asks for clarification; if response is incorrect, directs student to previous learning via prompt.	• Teacher poses question and asks for clarification when response is correct (e.g., How did you know? How do you figure that out?), but moves to direct explanation when response is incorrect.	• Teacher poses question, and when student(s) respond incorrectly, supplies the answer or moves on to next student.
Teacher differentiates instruction and practice based on formative assessment.	• Group formation is flexible and based on formative assessment from daily lessons. • Students are able to apply information based on the support provided by instruction. • Tasks differ based on students' needs and/or students' selection.	• Group formation is flexible, based on formative assessments from weekly lessons. • Students apply information based on initial instruction and teacher support.	• Group formation is based on recent formative assessments but is fixed. • Tasks are similar to those presented in lesson.	• Group formation is static and based on outdated information. • Tasks are identical for each group, with no visible differentiation.

Phase 3: Collaborative Learning

Quality Indicator	Proficient – 4	Skillful – 3	Approaching – 2	Minimal – 1
The tasks assigned accurately reflect the established purposes.	• All tasks students complete reflect the established purposes.	• Most tasks students complete reflect the established purposes.	• Some tasks students complete reflect the established purposes.	• Tasks students complete are not consistent with the stated purposes.
Students use strategies and skills that were previously modeled.	• After receiving adequate time in scaffolded instructional support, all students can complete tasks using the strategy or skill that was modeled.	• After receiving limited time in scaffolded instructional support, students complete tasks using the strategy or skill that was modeled.	• Students move directly to independent learning, with little in the way of instructional support.	• There is a mismatch between what was modeled and what students are asked to do.

Phase 3: Collaborative Learning (continued)

Quality Indicator	Proficient – 4	Skillful – 3	Approaching – 2	Minimal – 1
The task is appropriately complex. It is a novel application of a grade-level-appropriate concept and is designed so that the outcome is not guaranteed (a chance for productive failure exists).	• Task reflects purpose(s) and allows students an opportunity to use a variety of resources to creatively apply and extend their knowledge. • Students have an opportunity to experiment with concepts. The accountability matches the task type.	• Tasks provide opportunities for students to apply their knowledge, although the outcome is somewhat assured. The accountability matches the task type.	• The task is somewhat reflective of the purpose of the lesson, but there is little opportunity for student experimentation or innovation. • The accountability matches the task type.	• Task is an exact replication of what was modeled with no opportunity for student experimentation with concepts. • Accountability is nonexistent or inappropriate for the task.
Small groups of 2–5 students are purposefully constructed to maximize individual strengths without magnifying areas of need.	• Groups are flexible and change based on students' academic needs, content area, or interest.	• Purposeful heterogeneous grouping occurs. • Groups are primarily based on students' proficiency.	• Some heterogeneous grouping occurs, but homogeneous grouping practices dominate. • Decisions based on assessments are not apparent.	• Grouping practices are solely homogeneous and are done primarily for scheduling convenience.
Students use accountable talk to persuade, provide evidence, ask questions of one another, and disagree without being disagreeable.	• Students reach a better understanding or consensus based on evidence and opinions provided by others. • Students hold each member of the group accountable by using questioning strategies and evidence to persuade or disagree. • The conversation is respectful and courteous.	• Students ask for and offer evidence to support claims. However, members continue to maintain initial beliefs or positions about a topic without considering the arguments of others. • The conversation is generally respectful, but some members may not participate.	• There is a process in place for accountable talk. However, student dialogue is limited and there are minimal efforts to support statements, opinions, or claims. • The conversation is generally respectful, but is often dominated by one member of the group.	• No clear process is in place to facilitate accountable talk. Lack of structure is evidenced by students who are off task, in conflict, or unable to complete tasks.

(continued)

Figure 6.3   Gradual Release of Responsibility Quality Indicators—(continued)

Phase 4: Independent Learning

Quality Indicator	Proficient – 4	Skillful – 3	Approaching – 2	Minimal – 1
Tasks are meaningful, relevant, and an extension of the purposes for learning.	• Learning tasks provide opportunities to apply learning in unique or different situations that deepen students' learning. • The tasks are relevant and generate new questions for the learner.	• Learning tasks provide students with opportunities to apply what they have learned.	• Learning tasks mirror previous instruction rather than serve as an opportunity to apply what has been learned.	• Learning tasks are disconnected to instruction.
Teacher provides explicit feedback in order to deepen or solidify students' understanding.	• Feedback is timely, actionable, understandable, and specific. • Students are able to use feedback to improve and refine their learning. • Feedback is carefully crafted to focus on the processes used and to develop self-regulation and metacognition.	• Feedback is timely, understandable, and specific. • The feedback is carefully crafted to focus on the processes used and to develop self-regulation and metacognition. • Feedback occurs at the end of independent learning and cannot be used to improve and refine learning.	• Feedback is timely and understandable, but more general. • The feedback is primarily focused on the task, rather than processes, self-regulation, and metacognition. • Feedback occurs at the end of independent learning and cannot be used to improve and refine learning.	• Feedback is focused exclusively on correction. It may be delayed, misunderstood, and/or vague. • Feedback occurs too late to be useful in promoting student learning.
Students assume increased responsibility for learning.	• Students self-evaluate their learning and develop next steps to increase their understanding of the content.	• Students routinely self-evaluate their learning as a reflective process rather than a proactive one.	• Students discuss their learning with peers or teacher but do not routinely self-evaluate.	• Teacher provides feedback, but students do not have time to evaluate their learning.

and completing independent reading assignments. After we introduce each activity, we divide the students into groups so they can practice it. For example, after we have taught two collaborative learning activities, we split the class in half and ask each group to complete a task, and then switch. We spend our time circulating and assisting, monitoring behavior, and redirecting students who are off task. As we introduce new collaborative and independent tasks, we further subdivide the class. Once we have taught the major tasks, including routines and procedures, we then introduce guided instruction into the mix. Only when students have been properly prepared for collaborative and independent learning can you count on having the (relatively) uninterrupted time you'll need for small-group guided instruction.

Do I have the materials I need to engage my students?

This question relates to differentiated instruction, as you'll discover that your students need a range of materials in order to learn the content. The textbook is a great resource, but it is not the only item students should have. Bookmark websites on your classroom computers, curate resources to post on your learning management system, and talk to your media specialist about print and digital materials. We have worked at schools where grade levels assemble "resource kits" of specialized materials, which are stored in labeled boxes and available for checkout. These resource kits are great, because they encourage all of us to dig out materials we use only once a year. You may find that you need multiple copies of some supplies, such as file folder games for young children or storage bags of math manipulatives. Elementary schools are fortunate in being able to draw on the support of family volunteers to complete this kind of project. If you are working at a middle or high school, consider promoting the creation of resource kits as a community service project for an honor society, a school club, or a young adult who is fulfilling requirements for a scholarship, diploma, or degree. More recently, these resource kits can be made completely digital to support online learning.

Where can I find more time for guided instruction?

You can't create more time, but you can use the time you have more effectively. A great tip is to look for occasions when what you're doing is more managerial than instructional—when you are showing a video in class, for example, or supervising independent work, watching students as they read an assignment, or walking up and down the aisles of the classroom, hushing students as you go. If you recast whole-class activities that don't require your active participation to be collaborative tasks, you'll be free to spend more of your time providing guided instruction to small groups.

What can I do to ensure that independent learning tasks really are meaningful?

Like us, you probably vowed in your teacher preparation program that you would never be one of "those" teachers who gives students lots of busywork as a way to maintain order (meaning silence) in the classroom. We hope we have made a case that independent learning tasks are a critical component of a gradual release of responsibility model, but we also feel teachers really do need to examine the quality of what is traditionally used for independent work. Problem sets and questions at the end of the chapter are rarely engaging enough to keep most learners motivated. These practice-level tasks can be made more interesting by shifting them to the collaborative learning phase, giving students an opportunity to use the social and academic language they need in order to support their own learning.

Wilson and Cutting (2001) remind us that students advance their learning in the following ways:

- *Finding out:* Tasks associated with Bloom's knowledge and comprehension levels
- *Sorting out:* Tasks associated with the application and analysis levels
- *Speaking out:* Tasks associated with the synthesis and evaluation levels

Although all of these levels of understanding are important, we view synthesis and evaluation as the most essential to lasting understanding. If students' independent learning tasks are clumping up at the "finding out" and "sorting out" categories to the exclusion of "speaking out" opportunities, this is a signal that you should shift those tasks to other phases of the framework: to focus lessons, guided instruction, or collaborative learning.

What classroom routines and procedures will help me teach this way?

Routines and procedures are essential in any physical or digital classroom, regardless of the age of the students or the teacher's instructional approach. There should be clear routines for retrieving and putting away supplies, for example, and for submitting completed work and asking for help. In a gradual release of responsibility classroom, routines and procedures for the following tasks would prove particularly useful:

- Following schedules for collaborative learning and guided instruction groups
- Transitioning between whole-group and small-group learning
- Maintaining an acceptable noise level
- Wrapping up at the end of class, such as writing down homework assignments and completing online exit tickets

Conclusion

The gradual release of responsibility instructional framework is not something that can be implemented overnight, but it can be adopted and applied more and more successfully over time. This approach complements other research-based strategies, especially differentiated instruction, the backward planning of UbD, and social and emotional learning.

Consider the necessary routines and procedures that students will need to know, and then dedicate some time each day to providing instruction on how to work collaboratively and independently. This will make the introduction of guided instruction much smoother, because students will know what is expected from them, even when you aren't standing in front of them to tell them explicitly.

As you prepare to close this book (and, we hope, share it with a colleague), reconsider how *you* learn. Think about the things you're good at and about how you got good at them. Can you see the gradual release of responsibility instructional framework in your own learning? Can you see this approach resulting in better outcomes for students?

The responsibility is now yours... enjoy it.

References

Aldrich, C. (2005). *Learning by doing: A comprehensive guide to simulations, computer games, and pedagogy in e-learning and other educational experiences.* San Francisco: Jossey-Bass.

Anderson, N. J. (2002, April). *The role of metacognition in second language teaching and learning* (ERIC Digest EDO-FL-01-10). Retrieved from http://www.cal. content/download/1560/16583/file/RoleofMetacognitioninSecondLanguag-eTeachingandLearning.pdf

Atkinson, R. C., & Shiffrin, R. M. (1968). Human memory: A proposed system and its control processes. *Psychology of Learning and Motivation, 2,* 89–195.

Bandura, A. (1965). Influence of models' reinforcement contingencies on the acquisition of imitative responses. *Journal of Personality and Social Psychology, (6)1,* 589–595. doi:org/10.1037/h0022070

Bandura, A. (2006). Toward a psychology of human agency. *Perspectives on Psychological Science, 1,* 164–180.

Benjamin, A. (2002). *Differentiated instruction: A guide for middle and high school teachers.* Larchmont, NY: Eye on Education.

Burke, J. (2002). *Tools for thought: Graphic organizers for your classroom.* Portsmouth, NH: Heinemann.

Cain, S. (2012). *Quiet: The power of introverts in a world that can't stop talking.* New York: Broadway Paperbacks.

Choppin, J. (2011). The impact of professional noticing on teachers' adaptations of challenging tasks. *Mathematical Thinking and Learning, 13*(3), 175–197. doi:10.1080/10986065.2010.495049

Collins, A., Brown, J. S., & Newman, S. E. (1989). Cognitive apprenticeship: Teaching the crafts of reading, writing, and mathematics. In L. B. Resnick

(Ed.), *Knowing, learning, and instruction: Essays in honour of Robert Glaser* (pp. 453–494). Hillsdale, NJ: Lawrence Erlbaum Associates.

Daniels, H. (2001). *Literature circles: Voice and choice in book clubs and reading groups.* York, ME: Stenhouse.

Daniels, H. (2006). What's the next big thing with literature circles? *Voices from the Middle, 13*(4), 10–15.

Désert, M., Préaux, M., & Jund, R. (2009). So young and already victims of stereotype threat: Socio-economic status and performance of 6 to 9 years old children on Raven's progressive matrices. *European Journal of Psychology of Education, 24*(2), 207–218.

Donovan, M. S., & Bransford, J. D. (2005). *How students learn: History, mathematics, and science in the classroom.* Washington, DC: National Research Council.

Duffy, G. G. (2009). *Explaining reading: A resource for teaching concepts, skills, and strategies* (2nd ed.). New York: Guilford.

Dufresne, A., & Kobasigawa, A. (1989). Children's spontaneous allocation of study time: Differential and sufficient aspects. *Journal of Experimental Child Psychology, 47*(2), 274–296. Retrieved from doi:10.1016/0022-0965(89)90033-7

Duke, R. A. (2012). Their own best teachers: How we help and hinder the development of learners' independence. *Music Educators Journal, 99*(2), 36–41. Retrieved from doi:10.1177/0027432112458956

Dweck, C. (2007). *Mindset: The new psychology of success.* New York: Ballantine Books

Dweck, C. S. (2010, September). Even geniuses work hard. *Educational Leadership, 68*(2), 16–20.

Ericsson, K. A., Krampe, R. T., & Tesch-Romer, C. (1993). The role of deliberate practice in the acquisition of expert performance. *Psychological Review, 100*(3), 363–406.

Falloon, G. (2020). From simulations to real: Investigating young students' learning and transfer from simulations to real tasks. *British Journal of Educational Technology, 51*(3), 778–797.

Fisher, A. T., Alder, J. G., & Avasalu, M. (1998). Lecturing performance appraisal criteria: Staff and student difference. *Australian Journal of Education, 42*(2), 153–168.

Fisher, D., & Frey, N. (2008). Homework and the gradual release of responsibility: Making "responsibility" possible. *English Journal, 98*(2), 40–45.

Fisher, D., & Frey, N. (2012). *Collaborative learning: Ensuring students consolidate understanding.* Newark, DE: International Literacy Association.

Fisher, D., & Frey, N. (2015). *Checking for understanding: Formative assessment techniques for your classroom* (2nd ed.). Alexandria, VA: ASCD.

Fisher, D., & Frey, N. (2019). *Improving adolescent literacy: Content area strategies at work* (5th ed.). Upper Saddle River, NJ: Pearson.

Fisher, D., Frey, N., & Almarode, J. (2020). *Student learning communities: A springboard for academic and social-emotional development.* Alexandria, VA: ASCD.

Fisher, D., Frey, N., Anderson, H., & Thayre, M. (2015). *Text-dependent questions: Pathways to close and critical reading, grades 6–12.* Thousand Oaks, CA: Corwin.

Fisher, D., Frey, N., & Pumpian, I. (2012). *How to create a culture of achievement in your school and classroom.* Alexandria, VA: ASCD.

Flavell, J. H. (1979). Metacognition and cognitive monitoring: A new area of cognitive-developmental inquiry. *American Psychologist, 34*(10), 906–911. Retrieved from soi:10.1037/0003-066X.34.10.906

Frey, N., & Fisher, D. (2011). *The formative assessment action plan: Practical steps to more successful teaching and learning.* Alexandria, VA: ASCD.

Frey, N., Fisher, D., & Gonzalez, A. (2010). *Literacy 2.0: Reading and writing in 21st century classrooms.* Bloomington, IN: Solution Tree.

Gonzalez, J. (2018, March 26). Frickin' packets [Blog post]. *Cult of Pedagogy.* Retrieved from https://www.cultofpedagogy.com/busysheets/

Graff, G., & Birkenstein, C. (2009). *They say/I say: The moves that matter in academic writing.* New York: Norton.

Guzzetti, B. J., Snyder, T. E., Glass, G. V., & Gamas, W. S. (1993). Promoting conceptual change in science: A comparative meta-analysis of instructional interventions from reading education and science education. *Reading Research Quarterly, 28*(2), 116–159. doi:10.2307/747886

Hattie, J. A. C. (2009). *Visible learning: A synthesis of over 800 meta-analyses relating to achievement.* New York: Routledge.

Hattie, J. A. C. (2013). Calibration and confidence: Where to next? *Learning and Instruction, 24,* 62–66. doi:10.1016/j.learninstruc. 2012.05.009

Hattie, J. A. C., Brown, G. T., & Keegan, P. (2005). A national teacher-managed, curriculum-based assessment system: Assessment tools for teaching & learning (asTTle). *International Journal of Learning, 10,* 770–778.

Hattie, J. A. C., & Donoghue, G. M. (2016). Learning strategies: A synthesis and conceptual model. *NPJ Science of Learning,* 1, article 16013. doi:10.1038/npjscilearn.2016.13

Hattie, J., & Timperley, H. (2007). The power of feedback. *Review of Educational Research, 77*(1), 81–112. doi:10.3102/003465430298487

Howard, J. L., Gagné, M., & Bureau, J. S. (2017). Testing a continuum structure of self-determined motivation: A meta-analysis. *Psychological Bulletin, 143*(12), 1346–1377.

International Society for Technology in Education. (2012). *Advancing digital age learning.* Retrieved from http://www.iste.org/standards/nets-for-students

Kellough, R. D., & Kellough, N. G. (1999). *Secondary school teaching: A guide to methods and resources.* Upper Saddle River, NJ: Prentice Hall.

Kesten, C. (1987). *Independent learning.* Regina, Canada: Saskatchewan Education.

Kriegbaum, K., Becker, N., & Spinath, B. (2018). The relative importance of intelligence and motivation as predictors of school achievement: A meta-analysis. *Educational Research Review, 25,* 120–148.

Lee, I. (2009). Ten mismatches between teachers' beliefs and written feedback practice. *ELT Journal, 63*(1), 13–22. doi:org/10.1093/elt/ccn010

Marulis, L. L., Palincsar, A., Berhenke, A., & Whitebread, D. (2016). Assessing metacognitive knowledge in 3–5 year-olds: The development of a metacognitive knowledge interview (McKI). *Metacognition & Learning, 11,* 339–368.

McMahon, S. I., Raphael, T. E., Goatley, V. J., & Pardo, L. S. (2007). *The book club connection: Literacy learning and classroom talk*. New York: Teachers College Press.

Nathan, M. J., & Petrosino, A. (2003). Expert blind spot among preservice teachers. *American Educational Research Journal, 40*(4), doi:10.3102/00028312040004905

National Association of Colleges and Employers. (2012, June). More than half the class had internship/co-op experience. *Spotlight for Career Services Professionals.* Retrieved from http://www.naceweb.org/s06062012/intern-co-op-experience/?menuID=364&referal=knowledgecenter

Oczkus, L. (2018). *Reciprocal teaching at work: Powerful strategies and lessons for improving reading comprehension* (3rd ed.). Alexandria, VA: ASCD.

Osborne, J., & Dillon, J. (2010). How science works: What is the nature of scientific reasoning and what do we know about students' understanding? In J. Osborne & J. Dillon (Eds.), *Good practice in science teaching: What research has to say* (pp. 20–45). Berkshire, England: McGraw-Hill Education.

Palincsar, A. S., & Brown, A. L. (1984). Reciprocal teaching of comprehension-fostering and comprehension-monitoring activities. *Cognition and Instruction, 1*(2), 117–175. doi:10.1207/s1532690xci0102_1

Partnership for 21st Century Skills. (2009). *Framework for 21st century learning.* Retrieved from http://www.battelleforkids.org/networks/p21

Pearson, P. D., & Gallagher, G. (1983). The gradual release of responsibility model of instruction. *Contemporary Educational Psychology, 8,* 112–123.

Piaget, J. (1952). *The origins of intelligence in children.* New York: Norton.

Raphael, T. E., Highfield, K., & Au, K. H. (2006). *QAR now: A powerful and practical framework that develops comprehension and higher-level thinking in all students.* New York: Scholastic.

Resnick, L. (1995). From aptitude to effort: A new foundation for our schools. *Daedalus, 124*(4), 55–62.

Rosenshine, B. (2008). *Five meanings of direct instruction.* Center on Innovation & Improvement. Retrieved from http://www.centerii.org/search/Resources%5CFiveDirectInstruct.pdf

Shih, M. J., Pittinsky, T. L., & Ho, G. C. (2012). *Stereotype boost: Positive outcomes from the activation of positive stereotypes.* In M. Inzlicht & T. Schmader (Eds.), *Stereotype threat: Theory, process, and application* (pp. 141–156). New York Oxford University Press.

Short, D. J., Fidelman, C. G., & Louguit, M. (2012). Developing academic language in English language learners through sheltered instruction. *TESOL Quarterly, 46*(2), 334–361.

Singer, S. R., Hilton, M. L., & Schweingruber, H. A. (2006). *America's lab report: Investigations in high school science.* Washington, DC: National Research Council.

Smith, D., Fisher, D., & Frey, N. (2019). *All learning is social and emotional: Helping students develop essential skills for the classroom and beyond.* Alexandria, VA: ASCD.

Smith, T. (2014). Elementary science instruction: Examining a virtual environment for evidence of learning, engagement, and 21st century competencies. *Education Sciences, (1)*, 122–138.

Summers, J. J. (2006). Effects of collaborative learning in math on sixth graders' individual goal orientations from a socioconstructivist perspective.
Elementary School Journal, 106, 273–290.

Tomlinson, C. A. (2014). *The differentiated classroom: Responding to the needs of
all learners* (2nd ed.). Alexandria, VA: ASCD.

U.S. Department of Labor Office, Office of Disability Employment Policy. (2012).
Soft skills to pay the bills: *Mastering soft skills for workplace success.* Washington, DC: Author.

Van Ryzin, M. J., Roseth, C. J., & McClure, H. (2020). The effects of cooperative
learning on peer relations, academic support, and engagement in learning
among students of color. *Journal of Educational Research, 113*(4), 283–291.

Vatterott, C. (2018). *Rethinking homework: Best practices that support diverse
needs* (2nd ed.). Alexandria, VA: ASCD.

Vygotsky, L. S. (1962). *Thought and language.* Cambridge, MA: MIT Press.

Vygotsky, L. S. (1978). *Mind in society.* Cambridge, MA: Harvard University
Press.

Webb, N. M., Nemer, K. M., & Ing, M. (2006). Small-group reflections: Parallels
between teacher discourse and student behavior in peer-directed groups.
Journal of the Learning Sciences, 15(1), 63–119.

White, E. B. (1948). Death of a pig. *The Atlantic, 81*(1), 28–33.

Wiggins, G. (1998). *Educative assessment: Designing assessments to inform and
improve student performance.* San Francisco: Jossey-Bass.

Wiggins, G., & McTighe, J. (2005). *Understanding by Design* (2nd ed.). Alexandria, VA: ASCD.

Wilson, J., & Cutting, L. (2001). *Contracts for independent learning: Engaging students in the middle years.* Melbourne: Curriculum Corporation.

Wood, D., Bruner, J. S., & Ross, G. (1976). The role of tutoring in problem solving. *Journal of Child Psychology and Psychiatry, 17*(2), 89–100. doi:10.1111/j.
1469-7610.1976.tb00381

Index

The letter *f* following a page locator denotes a figure.

About the Authors

 **Douglas Fisher** is a professor of educational leadership at San Diego State University and a teacher leader at Health Sciences High & Middle College. He is the recipient of an International Reading Association William S. Grey citation of merit, an Exemplary Leader award from the Conference on English Leadership of NCTE, and a Christa McAuliffe Award for Excellence in Teacher Education. Along with Nancy Frey, Doug has published numerous articles on improving student achievement, and his books include *The Purposeful Classroom: How to Structure Lessons with Learning Goals in Mind; Enhancing RTI: How to Ensure Success with Effective Classroom Instruction and Intervention; Checking for Understanding: Formative Assessment Techniques for Your Classroom; How to Create a Culture of Achievement in Your School and Classroom,* and *Using Data to Focus Instructional Improvement.* He can be reached at dfisher@mail.sdsu.edu. Follow him on Twitter: @ DFISHERSDSU.

 **Nancy Frey** is a professor of educational leadership at San Diego State University and a teacher leader at Health Sciences High & Middle College. Before joining the university faculty, Nancy was a special education teacher in the Broward County (Florida) Public Schools, where she taught students at the elementary and middle school levels. She later worked for the Florida Department of Education on a statewide project for supporting students with disabilities in a general education curriculum. Nancy is a recipient of the Christa McAuliffe Award for Excellence in Teacher Education from the American Association of State Colleges and Universities and the Early Career Award from the Literacy Research Association. Her research interests include reading and literacy, assessment, intervention, and curriculum design. She has published many articles and a number of books on literacy and instruction, including *All Learning Is Social and Emotional; Your Students, My Students, Our Students: Rethinking Equitable and Inclusive Classrooms,* and *Building Equity: Policies and Practices to Empower All Learners.* She can be reached at nfrey@mail.sdsu.edu. Follow her on Twitter: @NancyFrey.

To learn more about Doug, Nancy, and their work, please visit www.fisherandfrey.com.

Related ASCD Resources: Teaching

At the time of publication, the following resources were available (ASCD stock numbers in parentheses):

Gradual Release of Responsibility in the Classroom (Quick Reference Guide) by Douglas Fisher and Nancy Frey (#QRG116083)

Improving Student Learning One Teacher at a Time, 2nd Ed. by Jane E. Pollock and Laura J. Tolone (#117013)

Intentional and Targeted Teaching: A Framework for Teacher Growth and Leadership by Douglas Fisher, Nancy Frey, and Stefani Arzonetti Hite (#116008)

Learning That Sticks: A Brain-Based Model for K–12 Instructional Design and Delivery by Bryan Goodwin with Tonia Gibson and Kristin Rouleau (#120032)

How to Differentiate Instruction in Academically Diverse Classrooms, 3rd Ed. by Carol Ann Tomlinson (#117032)

Never Work Harder Than Your Students and Other Principles of Great Teaching, 2nd Ed. by Robyn R. Jackson (#1180340)

Rise to the Challenge: Designing Rigorous Learning That Maximizes Student Success by Jeff C. Marshall (#120007)

So Each May Soar: The Principles and Practices of Learner-Centered Classrooms by Carol Ann Tomlinson (#118006)

Student Learning Communities: A Springboard for Academic and Social-Emotional Development by Douglas Fisher, Nancy Frey, and John Almarode (#121030)

Teaching for Deeper Learning: Tools to Engage Students in Meaning Making by Jay McTighe and Harvey F. Silver (#120022)

Teaching Students to Become Self-Determined Learners by Michael Wehmeyer and Yong Zhao (#119020)

For up-to-date information about ASCD resources, go to www.ascd.org. You can search the complete archives of *Educational Leadership* at www.ascd.org/el.

For more information, send an email to member@ascd.org; call 1-800-933-2723 or 703-578-9600; send a fax to 703-575-5400; or write to Information Services, ASCD, 1703 N. Beauregard St., Alexandria, VA 22311-1714 USA.

WHOLE CHILD
TENETS

The ASCD Whole Child approach is an effort to transition from a focus on narrowly defined academic achievement to one that promotes the long-term development and success of all children. Through this approach, ASCD supports educators, families, community members, and policymakers as they move from a vision about educating the whole child to sustainable, collaborative actions.

Better Learning Through Structured Teaching relates to the **engaged, supported,** and **challenged** tenets. *For more about the ASCD Whole Child approach, visit* **www.ascd.org /wholechild.**

1 **HEALTHY**
Each student enters school healthy and learns about and practices a healthy lifestyle.

2 **SAFE**
Each student learns in an environment that is physically and emotionally safe for students and adults.

3 **ENGAGED**
Each student is actively engaged in learning and is connected to the school and broader community.

4 **SUPPORTED**
Each student has access to personalized learning and is supported by qualified, caring adults.

5 **CHALLENGED**
Each student is challenged academically and prepared for success in college or further study and for employment and participation in a global environment.